Contents

Community Leadership and Representation: Unlocking the Potential

The report of the Working Party
on the Internal Management of
Local Authorities in England:
July 1993

London: HMSO

Part I

Introduction

1.1 On 21 March 1991 Mr Michael Heseltine, Secretary of State for the Environment, announced that as a part of his general review of local government in England he intended to re-examine the internal management arrangements of local authorities to seek ways to improve the efficiency and effectiveness of their decision-making processes; and to enhance and improve the role of elected members.

1.2 In July 1991 the Department of the Environment published a consultation paper — *The Internal Management of Local Authorities in England*. Over 600 responses were received. Mr Michael Howard, then Secretary of State, announced on 26 June 1992 the establishment of a joint Working Party with the three main local authority associations, the Audit Commission, The Local Government Management Board and others to consider current practice and suggestions for improving internal management arrangements, and to investigate possible experimental models. Annex A lists the members of the Working Party. Annex B summarises the consultation paper and the responses to it.

1.3 The Secretary of State gave us a remit to:

— **consider the suggestions for improving internal management arrangements which were received in response to the consultation paper;**

— **consult individual authorities supporting new management models;**

— **work up detailed options suitable for trial by volunteering authorities, including adequate safeguards to protect minority parties and to secure value for money and propriety; and**

— **draw up a list of changes to primary and secondary legislation that would be necessary to enable such experiments to take place.**

1.4 We were anxious to hear as wide as possible a cross-section of views from local government, particularly the views of individual authorities which had either introduced new management models or were proposing to do so. We appointed

1

a small task force to visit a number of authorities which had adopted a range of internal management practices within the existing legislation or had proposed options for experimental models which would require legislative changes.

1.5 The task force sought to meet, amongst others, the leaders of the majority and minority parties, the chairmen and women of the main committees, the chief executive, the monitoring officer and other chief officers, 'backbench' councillors and users of local authority services, and local societies representing trade and commerce, or voluntary groups. In some authorities it also met members and officers of parish and town councils. In advance of its visit the task force circulated a questionnaire which set out the areas it would cover during its visit. A copy is at Annex C.

1.6 We were very grateful for all the help and advice given to us. We should thank in particular Professor John Stewart and colleagues at INLOGOV; Professor Ken Young at Queen Mary and Westfield College, University of London; John Harwood, the Chief Executive of Oxfordshire County Council; all the councillors who attended the seminar on 29 March ; and the councillors, officers and other people we met in all the authorities we visited. A complete list of these acknowledgements is at Annex D. Annex E lists the authorities visited by the task force.

1.7 All the members of the Working Party would like to record our gratitude to the secretary, Steven Watts, particularly for heading the task force in all its visits.

Part II

Foreword and Summary of Recommendations

2.1 The political management of local government, usually referred to as its internal management, is an issue which has been addressed on a number of occasions in the past 26 years, most notably in the Maud (1967), Bains (1972) and Widdicombe (1986) reports. Since then many authorities have been able to streamline their internal management arrangements. The legislative framework, adapted and amended, has proved sufficiently flexible to permit considerable scope for innovation by individual authorities.

2.2 People might, therefore, reasonably ask why if such a degree of flexibility does exist, and is being used by local authorities, this issue needs to be considered again now.

2.3 In all areas of the public sector new management styles are being developed to deal with new roles and new circumstances. Local government is at the forefront of these changes. In particular local government has had to respond to the increasing range and diversity of provision, with more contracting out of services, the creation of companies to provide services and the establishment of other institutional forms. This diversity of provision opens up opportunities for more choice and improved services. The local authority has to look not only to its traditional role as provider of services but also to one where the emphasis is now more on specifying requirements, co-ordinating functions and monitoring performance. The existing committee structure and many features of common practice grew up as the best ways of managing service provision: it may not be the best way of running an authority, with a new role, in the twenty-first century.

2.4 We therefore considered what another study of internal management should seek to achieve. In our view internal management of a local authority should secure in effective ways:

❖ leadership in the community;

❖ effective representation of the citizen;

❖ clear accountability;

3

- ❖ effectiveness in decision-making and implementation;
- ❖ effective scrutiny of policy and performance; and
- ❖ responsiveness to local people.

2.5 The case for improving internal management is that this will enable existing councillors to carry out their roles as decision-makers and community representatives more effectively and thus with more personal satisfaction, and will encourage more people to wish to become councillors. They should not be faced with incomprehensible bureaucracy, financial hardship or unnecessarily long hours in meetings which purport to take decisions which in reality have been taken elsewhere. People should be able to see what their councillors are doing, and should be able to influence decisions. They should have a right to efficient implementation of policies and service delivery. Each of these considerations is important irrespective of whether a single party holds a majority on an authority or — as is more common — two or more parties co-operate either formally or informally to provide political direction.

2.6 We therefore identified two main objectives for our review:

(i) **to strengthen the role of all elected members** in formulating council strategies, leading and representing their communities, and, within their powers, acting as consumer champions to help citizens in the area get the quality of services which is their right and hold to account those responsible for providing those services; and

(ii) **to develop the framework for effective leadership within local authorities** — including clear political direction, identifying the needs and priorities of local communities and overseeing the efficient provision of high quality services to them.

2.7 To these ends we believe it is important to acknowledge the reality of the part the political group can play both where there is a majority administration and in councils where there is no overall control; to reduce the focus of attention by councillors on detailed administration to enable them to concentrate on stategic issues; to ensure that councillors are adequately trained and receive adequate support to fulfil their duties; to ensure that the system of allowances is adequate; and to look at ways of decentralising procedures to involve local people.

2.8 Such developments are necessary to unlock potential: to ensure that people who would make good councillors are not unnecessarily deterred, that members of the public can easily participate in local issues, that councils make their decisions with the minimum of bureaucracy; and that they can carry out an effective leadership role in their local communities.

2.9 In this report, on the basis of current good practice in internal management, we examine the issues local authorities should consider when they review and develop their arrangements within the existing legislative framework; how the councillors' allowances system could be reformed and administrative support be provided to encourage the widest possible range of people to participate in local government; and what new executive models might be adopted so as to further streamline political management of local authorities. We make recommendations which we hope will secure the objective of unlocking the potential of individuals and authorities to represent and lead their communities.

2.10 We deliberately do not identify an ideal internal management model and recommend its application as a blueprint to all local authorities. We recognise that different approaches will be appropriate for different authorities, and that it is for them and not central government to choose which arrangements to adopt. We do however urge all authorities to review their current practice to see whether they can do more to achieve the objectives we have identified.

Summary of Main Recommendations

2.11 We recommend:

1. **That all local authorities should review their internal management arrangements to assess whether or not they are the most appropriate ones to achieve the objectives set out in paragraph 2.6 of this report. Shadow or new unitary authorities should also ensure that they design appropriate internal management arrangements.**

2. **That the local authority associations should disseminate good practice in internal management, encouraging innovation and diversity, and should, amongst other things:**

(a) commission written material on how to maximise the flexibility that exists within the current legislative framework; issues which councils should be invited to address should include:

   (i) the role of the policy committee and full council in giving strategic guidance;

   (ii) the establishment of scrutiny and review committees to scrutinise and review policy formulation and performance;

   (iii) the enhancement of the role of the councillor as representative and champion of his or her community;

   (iv) the most effective use of the committee system, and of full council, by setting clear and meaningful agendas, varying the nature and purpose of committee meetings within a sensible cycle of business, and timing meetings so as to encourage maximum participation by councillors and citizens; and

   (v) decentralisation of the decision-making process to the lowest practical level.

(b) develop training programmes for councillors, both on general issues relating to their duties, responsibilities and opportunities, and on technical and administrative aspects of their roles as councillors;

(c) advise local authorities of ways in which administrative assistance and other support should be provided for councillors as members of an executive and in their constituency role; and

(d) illustrate ways of providing better quality information to councillors to assist them in their responsibilities as leaders of their communities, ward or divisional representatives, and as consumer champions.

3.   That, in order to ensure that people with a wide range of backgrounds are encouraged to serve as councillors, the Government should review, clarify and, as necessary, amend the allowances system to:

(a)   give local authorities greater discretion over what allowances to pay and to whom: there should be a substantial increase in the headroom within which each authority has the discretion to incur expenditure on allowances and the government should specify only a minimum basic allowance to be paid to all members;

(b)   remove the upper limit on the payment of special responsibility allowances;

(c)   make specified single party meetings and single member duties eligible for payment of allowances;

(d)   require a report to be published each year on the operation of the scheme and on the level of payments to individual members;

(e)   review the interaction of the social security benefits' and allowances' systems;

(f)   review the operation of the travel and subsistence allowances' scheme with a view to bringing the levels paid to officers and to councillors into alignment;

(g)   review the powers local authorities have to meet the costs of services provided to members which enable them to carry out their duties as councillors; and

(h)   consider the restoration of the financial loss allowance for councillors.

4.   That the Secretary of State for the Environment should take powers to allow, in consultation with local government, experimental changes to their internal management arrangements proposed by individual local authorities; legislation would allow approval of experiments including the following ingredients, amongst others, subject to suitable safeguards:

(a)   the replacing of the existing committee structure and the introduction of executive models and other structures of political management;

(b)   the creation of deliberative committees whose membership consisted only of members of the majority group (or dominant coalition group);

(c)   the decentralisation of decision-taking;

(d)   new rights for councillors to review and scrutinise council decisions; and

(e) enhanced roles for councillors not in executive positions.

5. **That for this purpose the Secretary of State should appoint a panel of advisers to consider each application put to him for consent to establish an experimental model; the membership of the panel should include nominees from the DOE, the local authority associations, the Audit Commission and The Local Government Management Board.**

6. **That where experimental models are approved they should be subject to annual review by the advisory panel, which should publish annual reports. The Secretary of State should have powers to suspend or modify an experimental model or models where the panel reported they were failing; and, after a period of time to be determined the panel should evaluate the experimental models and make appropriate recommendations to the Secretary of State about their possible wider application in authorities which wished to adopt them, or their continuation without time limit if the experimenting authority so wished.**

Part III

The Background

3.1 During the past 25 years there has been a continuing debate about the internal management arrangements of local authorities in England, and in the rest of the United Kingdom. This debate has reflected a general concern to protect and enhance the three essential characteristics of local government — its democracy, its openness and its accountability. In this section we set out a short history of local government management arrangements and comment on the three reports which have most influenced its development in recent years.

The Development of Internal Management Arrangements

3.2 By the beginning of the twentieth century, multi-purpose elected county and county borough councils, urban and rural district councils and metropolitan boroughs in London had been created, and had formed committees to run the services they had inherited from a variety of predecessor bodies. The powers of authorities to form committees were standardised in the Local Government Act 1933 and have remained much the same ever since. The discretion to delegate decisions to committees and sub-committees was substantially widened in the Local Government Act 1972.

3.3 The committee structure was originally focused on specific services. Since the 1970s many local authorities have increasingly sought to devise arrangements to enable them to take a more co-ordinated and strategic view of a council's responsibility. Most local authorities have established committees which are responsible for overall council policy. Since the 1974 reorganisation most councils have, in one form or another, established a policy and resources committee, which is expected to co-ordinate the work of specialised committees and focus on the use of resources — money, people and property. Since 1 August 1990, when the requirements of the Local Government and Housing Act 1989 for pro rata representation of political groups on committees came into force, minority groups have been able to obtain seats on all committees and sub-committees including such policy committees.

Changes to the Committee System

3.4 Changes to the committee system have been proposed in three major reports.

The Maud Report

3.5 The Committee on the Management of Local Government was established in 1964. It had a remit to consider how local government might best continue to attract and retain people — elected representatives and principal officers — of the calibre necessary to ensure its maximum effectiveness.

3.6 The Committee concluded that the country did not receive full value for money for the large expenditure on local government and identified three main causes:

(i) the survival of the nineteenth century tradition, enshrined in the committee system, that members must be concerned with the details of the day-to-day administration, with the result that officers were insufficiently trusted to take action without reference to members; in the Committee's view this practice was inefficient;

(ii) Parliament, ministers and government departments had increasingly lost faith in the responsibility of locally elected bodies, which deterred people of the required calibre from standing for election as members of councils. The Committee took the view that to ensure democracy, Government had to give local authorities a larger measure of home rule; and

(iii) there was often too wide a gulf in local government between the governors and the governed.

3.7 In 1967 the Committee recommended that local authorities should conduct a radical review of their internal organisation bearing the following points in mind:-

— there should be a clear division between member and officer;

— council members should exercise sovereign power within the authority and accept responsibility for everything done in the council's name, but having settled the policy should delegate to officers all but the most important decisions;

— committees should cease to be executive or administrative bodies, save for some exceptional purposes, and their main function should be deliberative;

— there should be as few committees as possible, perhaps no more than half a dozen even in large authorities; and each committee should concern itself with specific subjects;

— there should be as few sub-committees as possible;

— all but the smallest authorities should appoint a management board of between five and nine council members, and delegate wide powers to it;

— this board should be the sole channel by which business done in committee reaches the council and should itself formulate and present proposals requiring council approval, and propose the establishment and disestablishment of committees: it would serve as the focal point for management of the authority and supervise the work of the authority as a whole;

— if the council were organised on party political lines, the minority party should be offered representation on the management board; and

— a council should be free to pay members of its management board a part-time salary in addition to any allowance payable to ordinary council members.

3.8 Not all of the Committee's recommendations were adopted. Sir Andrew Wheatley, Clerk to the Hampshire County Council, explained in his note of dissent that the Committee's proposals 'left far too much power in the hands of a small number of members who will be members of the management board, and will deprive the great majority of the members of the council of the opportunity of participating effectively in the formulation of policy and the development of services'. For like-minded Sir Norman Chester, Warden of Nuffield College, most members would have 'little or no responsibility — only to criticise and be active at council meetings — a pleasant but not very responsible activity' while committees would be so downgraded as to make it unlikely that councillors would want to serve on them.

3.9 We have been struck by the similarity between those arguments put to the Maud Committee in the Sixties and the debate that continues in the Nineties. In our view much of the Maud Committee's analysis remains relevant today.

Bains Report

3.10 In 1971 the Study Group on Local Authority Structures was established under the chairmanship of the then Sir Frank Marshall. The Working Group which it established was chaired by Malcolm Bains, Clerk to Kent County Council. Its remit was to help the local authorities to be established in 1974 in determining their structures of management for elected member and officers. Its areas of interest included the roles of elected members and officers and the functions of committees and sub-committees.

3.11 The Study Group report made few specific recommendations but drew general conclusions about the challenges then facing local government. It identified eight main themes:

(i) **the role of members and officers** — it would be necessary for officers and members to forge an effective partnership with mutual appreciation of their respective roles;

11

(ii) **the aims of the individual member** — the management structure should enable every member to find satisfaction in fulfilling their particular roles;

(iii) **monitoring and reviewing performance** — an area of activity identified by the Study Group as almost totally ignored in local government and one in which the member had a vital role;

(iv) **effective and efficient decision making** — required a logical pattern of delegation, especially to officers, with decisions taken at the lowest practical level;

(v) **the corporate approach** — the departmental approach was thought by the Study Group to be inappropriate: authorities had an overall interest in the economic, cultural and physical wellbeing of their communities and should consult regularly with other local authorities and statutory organisations;

(vi) **policy and resources committee** — all authorities should set up such committees to set objectives, co-ordinate and control the carrying out of those objectives, and finally monitor and review performance;

(vii) **chief executive** — each authority should have a new post of chief executive free of all departmental responsibilities and acting as head of the paid service; and

(viii) **personnel** — authorities should promote a greater awareness of personnel management and appoint a personnel manager.

3.12 As with Maud, some of the Bains issues remain as topical now as they were then, even though the management models advocated seem somewhat over-prescriptive and inflexible.

The Widdicombe Report

3.13 In 1985 the Committee of Inquiry into the Conduct of Local Authority Business was established under the chairmanship of David Widdicombe QC, to inquire into practices and procedures governing the conduct of local authority business, with particular reference to the rights and responsibilities of elected members and the respective roles of members and officers. The Committee was invited to make any necessary recommendations for strengthening the democratic process.

3.14 Its main findings were as follows:

— that the increasing politicisation of local government had placed strains on the statutory framework, and that in particular there was uncertainty about the proper relationship between majority and minority parties, between councillors and their local party organisations, between councillors and officers, and between the council and the public; and

— the Committee had been impressed by the diversity of local government and the desire to promote best practice, but in some areas conventions had broken down and the rule of law needed to be reasserted.

3.15 Its recommendations were intended to limit the possibilities of abuse, although the Committee was under no illusions that it was possible to close every loophole by means of new laws.

3.16 In June 1986 the Committee's recommendations included:-

(a) the system of decision-making should remain one in which the council is a corporate body; decisions are taken openly by, or on behalf of, the whole council, without any separate source of executive authority; officers serve the council as a whole;

(b) membership of committees with delegated powers (but not of purely deliberative committees) should reflect the political composition of the full council;

(c) delegation of urgent decisions to chairs of committees should be allowed;

(d) there should not be co-optees with voting rights on decision-taking committees;

(e) there should be a new system of councillors' allowances;

(f) the attendance allowance and financial loss allowance should be replaced with the basic flat-rate allowance; and councils should draw up schemes for payment of special responsibility allowances;

(g) uniform arrangements should be introduced for the election of councillors by stipulating one councillor for every electoral ward/division and that the whole council should be elected every four years;

(h) the rights of the public and the press to attend the meetings and view the papers of deliberative committees should be disapplied.

3.17 The Government responded to the Committee's report in July 1988 and enacted recommendations (a) (b) and (d) to (f) above either wholly or in part in the Local Government and Housing Act 1989. It did not accept recommendations (c) and (h) and it extended the political balance rules to include deliberative committees, contrary to recommendation (b).

3.18 In this report we compare what is happening on the ground today with the intended results of these reports and of the 1989 Act.

Part IV ————————————————————————————————

Recent Practice and Innovation within the Existing Legislative Framework

4.1 We describe the current legislative framework in detail in Annex F. Within its constraints many local authorities, including those visited by the task force, have been innovative in seeking to establish more efficient and effective means of decision-taking and to strengthen the democratic process. To illustrate the scope for flexibility we outline, in paragraphs 4.3 to 4.9, different arrangements which can be operated within the existing statutory framework.

4.2 We have not sought to carry out an exhaustive survey but it is important to realise the diversity which has been achieved. We do not seek to evaluate the various schemes, merely to reflect current practice in certain authorities, and we are not recommending them as models other authorities should adopt. We want merely to illustate the very wide range of models which can be adopted within the existing flexibilities. Further examples of ways in which local authorities are introducing different management models are given in the booklets called *Getting On With It* published by The Local Government Management Board. In paragraphs 4.10 to 4.12 we list options which we believe authorities could usefully consider in more detail in reviewing their own arrangements. We recognise that many authorities have already addressed all or some of these issues and have, as a consequence, implemented changes to their management arrangements.

Informal Arrangements

4.3 By no means all of the internal management arrangements we have seen rely on being a part of the formally recognised committee structure. Many authorities have established informal single group policy committee which in practice acts as an executive, in that key decisions are made which are subsequently put to the formal committee for ratification. The committee is usually small in number and includes the leader, deputy leader and the main service committee chairmen or women, and other leading members. Although they continue to maintain their traditional political neutrality the chief executive and chief officers may, on an informal basis, attend by invitation either the whole meeting or those parts of the meeting at which their service responsibilities are discussed. Papers prepared for such meetings are not made available to other members of the majority group or to members of the minority groups. The meetings are not always formally minuted. Decisions tend to be reported on an informal ad hoc basis.

4.4 Often the deliberations of this informal committee are preceded or followed by consideration of the same issues by group meetings which all members of the controlling party or parties may attend; and in this way all members of the party or parties which form the administration may influence policy. We discuss the role of the political group and group leadership in paragraphs 5.5 to 5.9.

4.5 To complement these arrangements, some authorities have established non-executive panels. These can be either issue or service related, need not be politically balanced and may be chaired by minority party members; or the minority group may, unusually, have the majority of members. Such panels and groups may advise on policy issues or review and monitor performance. But they do not make decisions.

4.6 In authorities where no party has overall control, a wide range of informal arrangements exist. In some authorities the leaders of all of the parties have formed themselves into informal cabinets, which consider strategic or controversial issues; in others the largest minority party forms the administration but is, as a result of administrative conventions agreed between the parties, barred from forming an alliance with any other single party to form a majority and to take decisions, but must seek the agreement of all party or group leaders to each decision, prior to the committee process.

Formal Arrangements

4.7 Most local authority business is delegated to committees and sub-committees. Many authorities have restructured these systems to improve the quality of decision-making including by reducing the number of times any decision needs to be taken and thus reducing the time needed to take a decision and the time councillors must spend attending committees. Councils have wanted to ensure that a reduction in the numbers of committees and sub-committees would not also result in a reduction in the involvement of councillors generally in the formulation of policy and in operational decisions. A second objective has commonly been to devolve decisions to the lowest point in the political hierarchy at which they need to be taken. This has been done by establishing neighbourhood offices, area committees and other local community-based fora with varying degrees of autonomy, often with officer management structures reorganised on the same basis.

4.8 To ensure the appropriate depth of involvement of elected members and the proper scrutiny of the actions of a smaller number of committees, some authorities have established issue-related review or policy panels and performance and quality-related scrutiny committees. These may be similar to the informal non-executive panels described in paragraph 4.5 but membership of these formal committees is based on political proportionality.

4.9 Set out below are four examples of how these and similar changes have been made.

COUNCIL A

(i)   This council has decentralised its operations. It has been divided physically and administratively into area committees.

(ii)   Each area committee has its own office at which staff provide all local services. Programme and operational decisions have been devolved to the area committees. Membership of the committees includes all of the elected councillors to wards within each area. This can mean a minority group on the whole council may have political control of an area committee.

(iii) The area committees appoint service related sub-committees. Because the provisions of the Local Government (Committees and Political Groups) (Amendment) Regulations 1991 do not apply to area committees, the sub-committees can be single party.

Beneath this is another tier of representation — elected residents fora, which advise the area committees but are not involved in policy formulation, and have no executive function.

The Centre's Role

(iv)   Policy is determined at the centre by a central strategy committee. Membership of this committee comprises the Leader of the Council, the Deputy Leader, and the chairmen and women of the area committees — including areas which are controlled by the minority groups. The committee is serviced by officers of the council, as and when required.

(v)   The authority has retained the usual range of committees, including statutory ones such as education and social services, which along with the central strategy committee consider the allocation of resources and minimum service provision levels on an authority-wide basis. Each area committee can then decide whether or not it wishes to make provision of services above the minimum level set, subject to resources. If decisions, taken at area level, threatened outside sources of finance for the whole council, the area committee could be overruled by the centre.

Single Party Groups

(vi)   The authority also has a series of Boards. They are single party advisory groups which have officers as members. They are usually service or issue related — for example the budget, or homelessness.

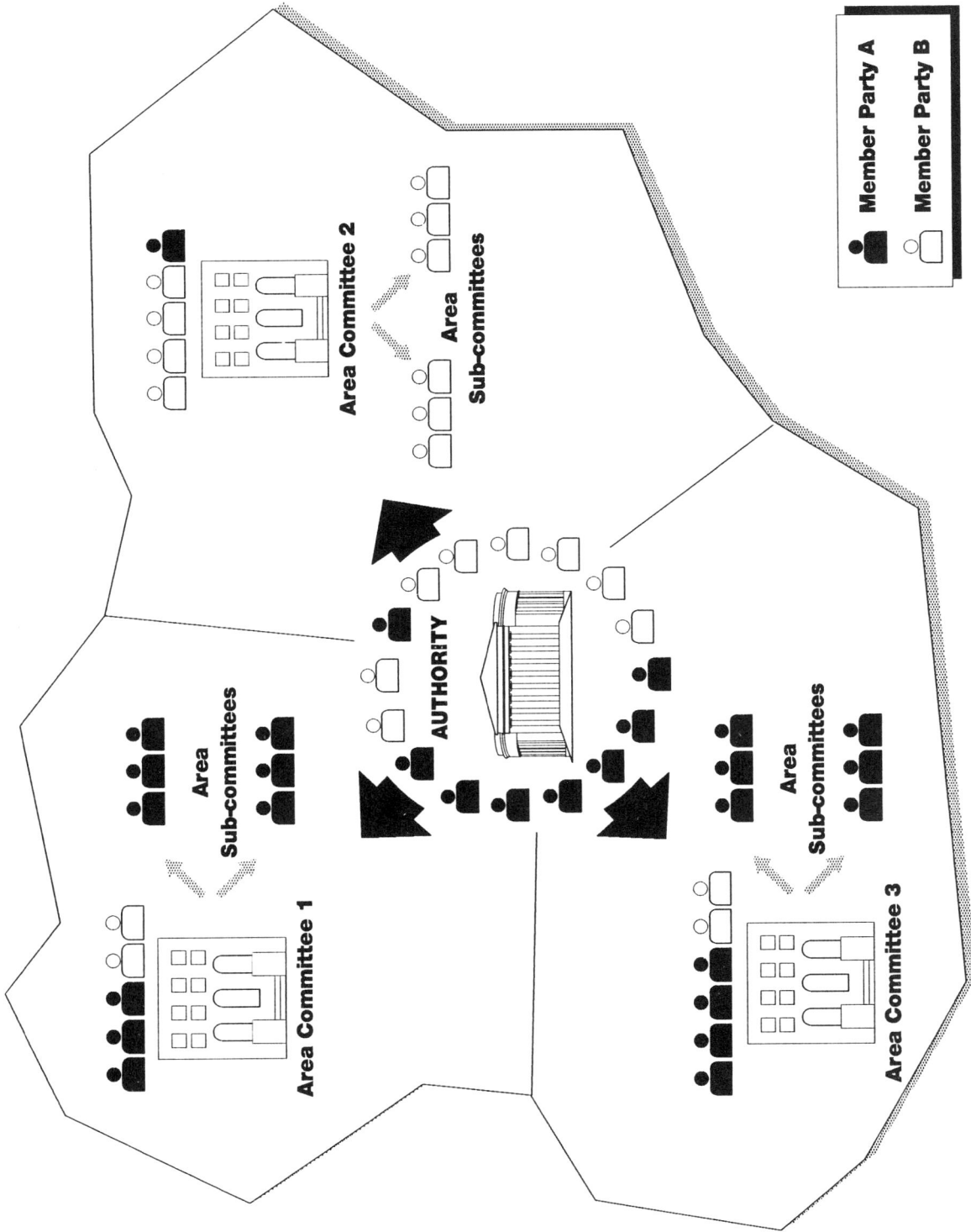

Area Committee 2

Area Sub-committees

AUTHORITY

Area Sub-committees

Area Committee 1

Area Sub-committees

Area Committee 3

Member Party A

Member Party B

COUNCIL B

(i)   The council has a Policy Committee which meets twice quarterly and has 15 members, including all of the chairmen and women of the service committees. The service committees meet quarterly. The service committees do not determine policy but determine priorities within agreed policies, set service standards and monitor service delivery. There are only eight sub committees.

(ii) Because there are so few sub-committees the authority has made other arrangements to enhance the involvement of councillors generally in policy formulation and in scrutinizing the actions of the council.

Service Advisory Groups (SAGs)

(iii) The council has established a series of ad hoc non-executive groups which offer advice and local feedback to chief officers on sensitive issues. There are usually five to eight members and they are not politically balanced — they may be chaired by a minority group member. Any proposals which a SAG wishes to put forward to a service committee or sub-committee must go through the appropriate chief officer — and it then becomes his recommendation.

Select Panels

(iv) The council has established a series of issue-related select panels. They address broad issues, and they are time-limited. Membership is politically balanced and attendance allowances are paid. Both the SAGs and the select panels are intended to be used to provide a more substantial role for members generally.

Political Direction

(v)   These arrangements are underpinned by an informal process of group meetings which usually precede the committee meetings. The majority group has constituted leading members as a 'Cabinet' which meets monthly to determine policy in detail. The group meetings set the agendas for the committee meetings. Minority group leaders are invited to regular meetings with the leader.

(vi) The Chief Executive attends the majority group meetings. Chief officers attend on request to deal with specific items, and attend regular meetings with the minority groups. A weekly information bulletin is prepared by officers for all councillors. Minority group members have free access to officers who brief them on a regular basis.

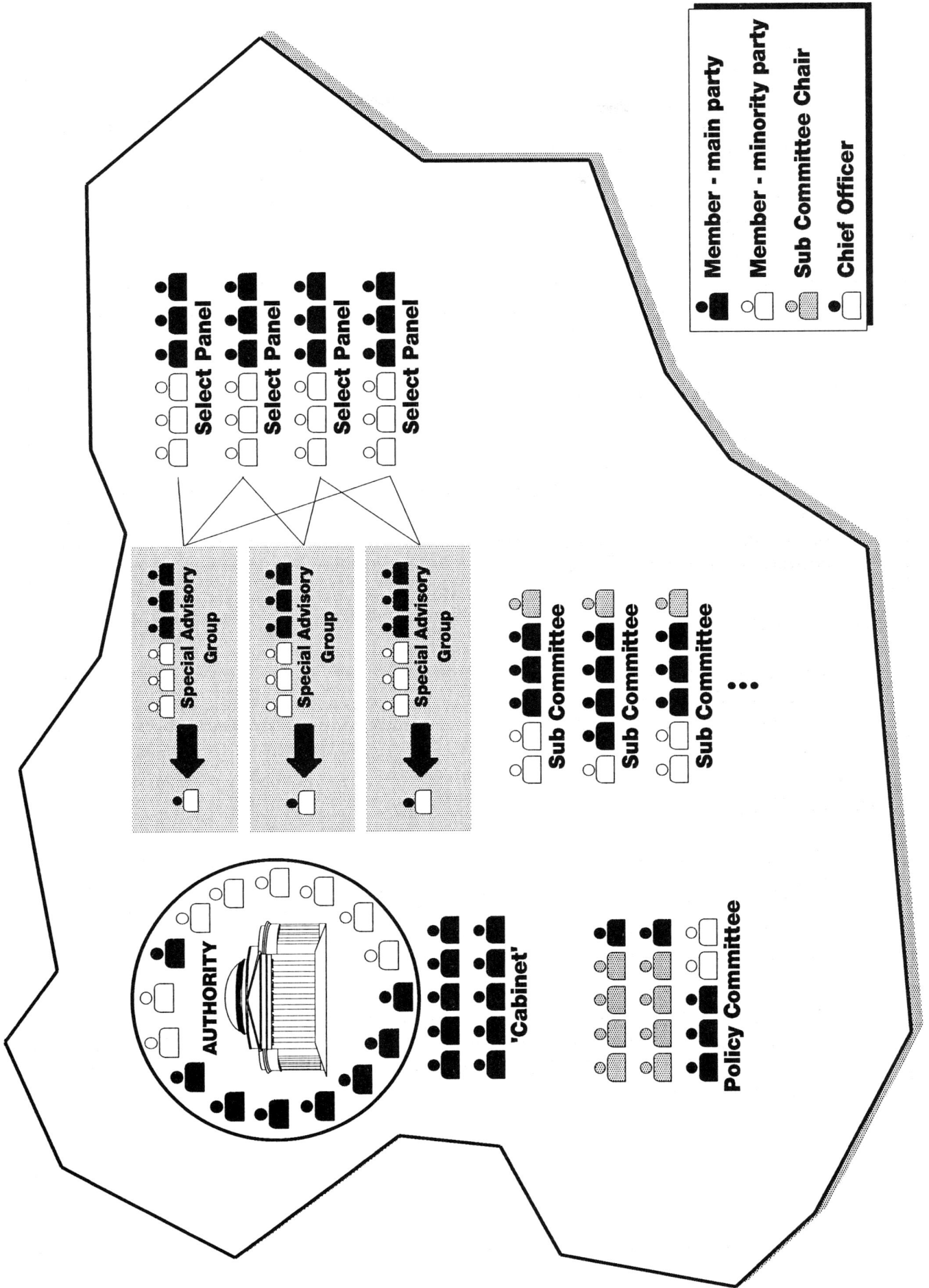

Select Panel

Select Panel

Select Panel

Select Panel

Special Advisory Group

Special Advisory Group

Special Advisory Group

Sub Committee

Sub Committee

Sub Committee

...

AUTHORITY

'Cabinet'

Policy Committee

Member - main party
Member - minority party
Sub Committee Chair
Chief Officer

COUNCIL C

(i)   The council has five committees — policy, social services, education, environment and police. Each committee has its own performance review panel. Six sub-committees deal with detailed policy areas and quasi judicial matters such as licensing. Overall there are only 50 formal committee meetings each year chaired by the majority party.

Performance Review Panels

(ii)   The performance review panels comprise 50% menbers from the related service committee and 50% non specialist members. They are usually, but not always, chaired by the majority party. Thier role is to scrutinise the effectiveness of policy and monitor performance

Policy Panels

(iii)   The authority has established a number of policy panels which are informal, task-specific and time-limited. They are not politically balanced and enable external parties including business and community organisations to become involved in policy discussion. A digest of the issues to be discussed by the panels is circulated to all members.

Community Government

(iv)   The council has established trial community government schemes in three areas. The objective is to give individual communities influence and a degree of control over their services and how they are delivered. In each area, local community groups — voluntary organisations, chambers of commerce, GP fora, members of town/parish/district/county councils, and staff from local services are invited by the council to meet and create a local agenda and determine local priorities. Currently this forum has neither executive powers nor resources. It is seen as reinforcing the constituency and representative role of the local councillor through the greater visibility and clarity of purpose of the local community. The council was not seeking to delegate powers of decision beyond issues whose impact was entirely local.

Political Direction

(v)   There is a Leader's Group consisting of the main committee chairs and the Leader. The Chief Executive also attends. This group acts as single party executive. Its meetings are confidential and other members do not have access to its papers or reports of its deliberations.

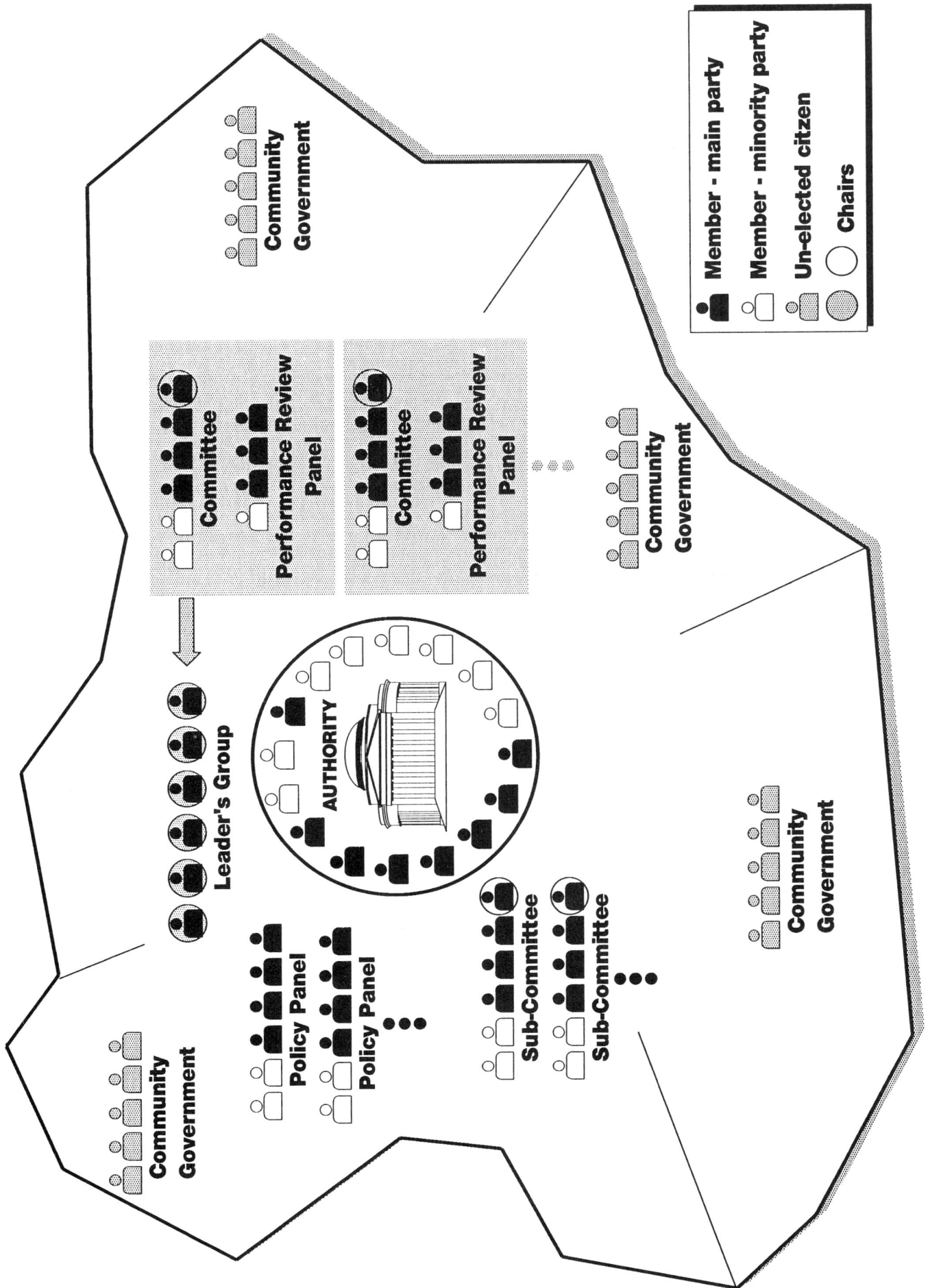

Community Government

Performance Review Panel

Committee

Performance Review Panel

Committee

Community Government

Leader's Group

AUTHORITY

Community Government

Policy Panel

Policy Panel

Sub-Committee

Sub-Committee

Community Government

Member - main party

Member - minority party

Un-elected citzen

Chairs

23

COUNCIL D

(i)   The council decided to restructure itself partly in response to the provisions of the Local Government & Housing Act 1989, but also to reflect the balanced nature of the council. Four parties are represented on the council.

Committee Structure

(ii)   There are four policy committees. They are supported by twenty service groups. All the committees and service groups are politically balanced and are chaired by members of the minority administration. Policy committees have 16-18 members and service groups 6-8. There is some overlap between policy committee and service group membership, e.g. chairs of service groups serve on the corresponding policy comittee.

(iii)   The Resources Policy Committee establishes and monitors the overall resources within which all services are to be provided, while the Direct Service Organisations Management Group, one of the service groups, monitors and advises on the specific allocation of resources to the DSOs. The council feels that the deployment of members on both of these bodies helps rather than hinders the interaction of client and provider.

(iv)   The service groups are developing their scrutiny role and to aid this they are being provided with performance indicators and regular papers on issues of service provision.

Political Direction

(v)   There is a Leader's Group which consists of the Leader and Secretary of each political party and the Chief Executive. It has no executive powers and is used only as a sounding board for testing the reaction to controversial issues before they are presented to the council.

(vi)   The Leader's Group, however, is not the forum within which the minority administration's policies are decided. Policies are set by the Management Board which comprises the Leader, Deputy Leader and the chairmen and women of the policy committees and the management team (the Chief Executive and four chief officers).

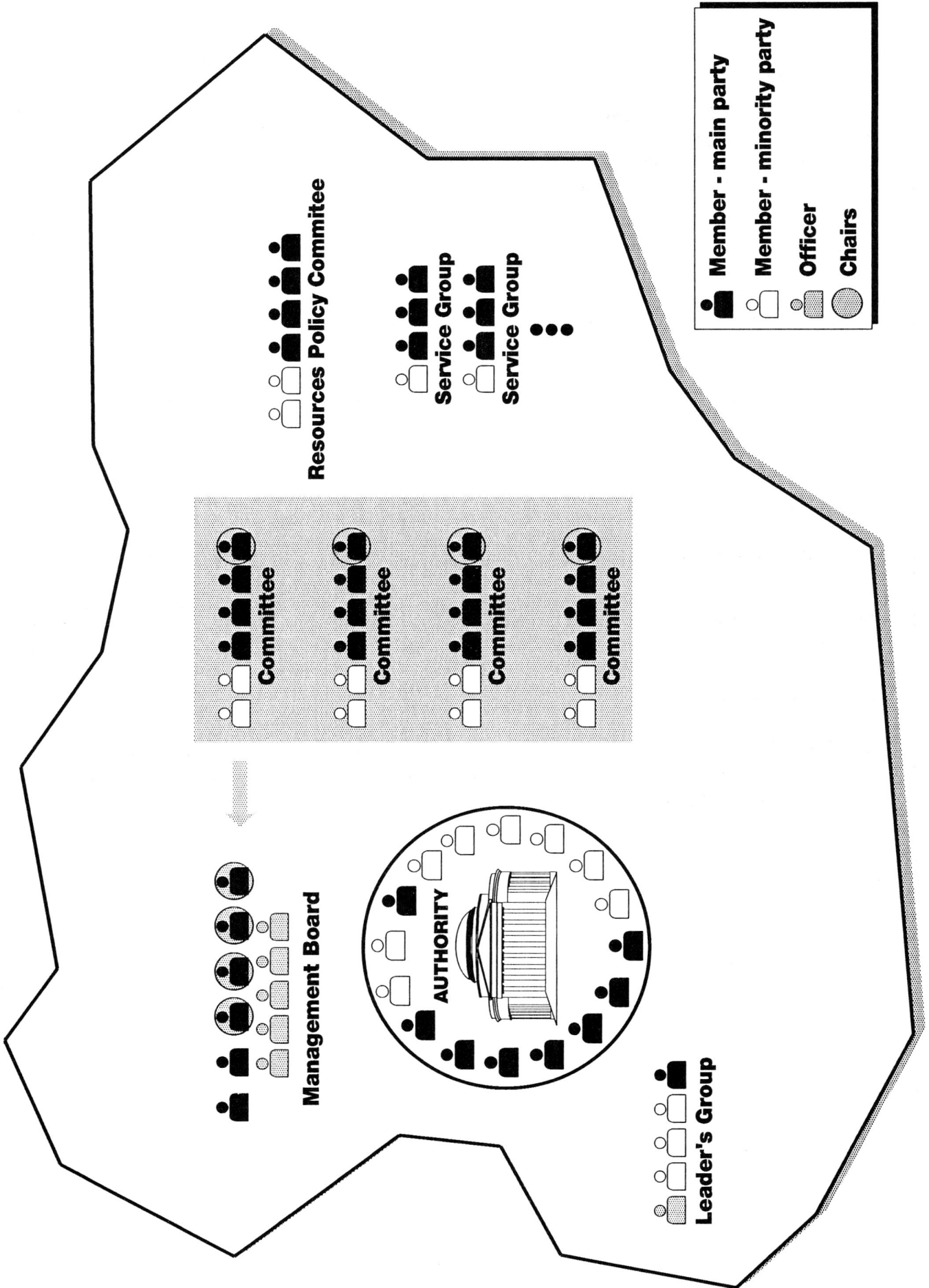

Resources Policy Committee

Service Group

Service Group

Committee

Committee

Committee

Committee

Management Board

AUTHORITY

Leader's Group

Member - main party
Member - minority party
Officer
Chairs

25

Options Within the Current Framework

4.10 We know that many councils do — and in our view, all councils should — regularly debate and review their internal management arrangements. Such reviews permit them to examine whether they could do more to achieve the objectives which we have identified, and whether different arrangements would be more fulfilling for present and future councillors and facilitate better quality service to local citizens. For example, the timing, content and frequency of the meetings which they hold can exclude the single parent, people with dependent relatives, the self-employed, night-shift workers, students, and others. Small changes to current practice can do much to improve the councillor's position and at the same time to make the authority a more effective leadership force.

4.11 We offer the following checklist of the sorts of issues some councils have addressed in reviewing their arrangements. Again we do not seek to imply there are single right solutions.

Strategic Direction

(i) Most authorities already have a policy committee which explicitly provides strategic direction to guide the running of the authority's affairs and sets out the authority's vision for local people. Other authorities need to use their policy committees specifically to identify what they want to achieve for their communities, and how it can be achieved. All authorities need a strategy for the services they provide themselves and for the services they wish to see provided to their communities by other agencies.

Community Leadership

(ii) Councillors can play an important role in monitoring the quality of services provided to their constituents by other agencies. Already some councils have developed a special forum where, for example, NHS representatives come in and give an account of health development and planning in the area and are subject to questioning. Other councils might find benefit in similar developments.

(iii) Many councillors find themselves invited to represent their authority on one or more outside bodies. This representation can provide an important opportunity for leadership and influence. Some councils provide support for those involved and opportunities for reporting back.

The Representative Role

(iv) The representative role of the councillor is indivisible from his or her role in policy formulation or the scrutiny of performance. The roles are mutually interdependent and inform each other. The representative role should be facilitated and encouraged. This has been done in some authorities by providing councillors with appropriate levels of support to carry out their duties and by taking steps to ensure they know in good time of issues affecting their constituencies and of the timing and method of the council's decision on them and providing them with adequate information about decisions and their impact on their areas. Some councils have enhanced the councillors' representative role by delegating operational decisions to neighbourhood or area committees, or have established such committees as advisory bodies.

Policy Development

(v) There are ways in which all councillors can become involved in the development of policy in their authorities, which need not necessarily take place only in the formal setting of committees or sub committees. Some authorities have established panels or working parties — on which officers and members are represented. Such panels may be issue or service-based and can provide informal advice on policy to the relevant service committees. Often they are ad hoc and time limited. They need not be politically balanced because they do not have executive powers. Because they are not formal committees of the council other individuals or representatives of organisations may be either co-opted as members or invited to give evidence or to present a case to the panel.

Policy Review

(vi) There is an equally important role for councillors in monitoring and reviewing the performance of their authorities in meeting predetermined performance standards and objectives. Again authorities have established panels or working parties, outside the formal committee structure, which review the delivery of services. The membership of such panels sometimes excludes members of the appropriate or related services committees, and minority groups are given either the chairmanship of the panel or the balance of membership is adjusted to give them a majority. This is seen to reassure the public of their independence and the legitimacy of their comments or advice.

The Role of the Full Council

(vii) The conventional role of the full council is largely formal, putting the seal of approval on decisions which have been taken elsewhere. Some councils have used the opportunity for changing this role to create a forum for general debate about local and national affairs. The full council meets more regularly with the agenda chosen by the different groups on a rota.

(viii) Other councils — and more may wish to — have adapted this forum to permit the participation of local members of the public — allowing them to make representations to its meetings or to take part in a question time. In this way the relationship between authorities and the citizens to whom they are accountable is being developed.

The Use and Timing of Meetings

(ix) The most common complaints we heard from councillors were not about the costs of being a councillor but about the time-consuming nature of their duties and the often unfocused nature of the debate in which they had to engage. Some councils have reorganised the timing of their meetings better to suit the needs of councillors and thus to ensure the maximum levels of attendance and participation; and others have considered differentiated use of meetings in different parts of the cycle — by emphasising different aspects of their role at different times — budget and policy framework, policy development and review, and general debate.

(x) Some councils have also addressed how they should structure their agenda and the clarity and quality of the information they provide. The quantity and style of paper, and the length of meetings, can significantly affect the quality of the councillor's life.

Administrative Support and Research Support

(xi) We were told that many authorities do not provide adequate administrative support either to members of the leadership groups or to other councillors. This undermines the ability of the councillor to fulfil his or her duties and in turn weakens the democratic process. Councillors should be provided with adequate support both in personnel and equipment and in particular should be provided with easy access to information about the performance of the authority and other agencies as it affects their division or ward and the authority as a whole.

(xii) It ought to be clear which costs incurred by councillors to carry out their duties are eligible for reimbursement by the council — for example the costs of installing fax machines or word processors in councillors' homes, telephone bills, and the costs of employing research assistants. We make a recommendation on this point at paragraph 4.23.

Training for New Councillors

(xiii) A very frequent complaint from councillors was that on election they had only a limited idea of what the role of councillors was and no one told them what to do, how to do it or how to use the council's resources. They were given the minimum assistance possible provided they turned up to the necessary meetings. Small wonder that some first-time councillors became quickly disenchanted. All councillors, old and new, should be offered full training and help through the administrative maze. In particular it should be made clear to them, through their parties or by officers, what their role is and what is expected of them, and they should be informed of the opportunities for them to play their part as division and ward representatives, in the policy formulation process, and as a reviewer/scrutineer.

4.12 Our hope is that if councils review their current practices along these lines, and in others too, they would make changes which would unlock the potential for individuals to participate as councillors: the potential for councillors to represent the interests of their constituents within the authority and more widely, and the potential for the authority to develop its role as the focus for its community.

4.13 We recommend that:

All local authorities should review their internal management arrangements to assess whether or not they are the most appropriate ones to achieve the objectives set out in paragraph 2.6 of this report. Shadow or new unitary authorities should ensure that they design appropriate internal management arrangements.

The local authority associations should disseminate good practice in internal management, encouraging innovation and diversity, and should, amongst other things:

(a) commission written material on how to maximise the flexibility that exists within the current legislative framework; issues which councils should be invited to address should include:

   (i) the role of the policy committee and full council in giving strategic guidance;

   (ii) the establishment of scrutiny and review committees to scrutinise and review policy formulation and performance;

   (iii) the enhancement of the role of the councillor as representative and champion of his or her community;

   (iv) the most effective use of the committee system, and of full council, by setting clear and meaningful agendas, varying the nature and purpose of committee meetings within a sensible cycle of business, and timing meetings so as to encourage maximum participation by councillors and citizens; and

   (v) decentralisation of the decision-making process to the lowest practical level.

(b) develop training programmes for councillors, both on general issues relating to their duties, responsibilities and opportunities, and on technical and administrative aspects of their roles as councillors;

(c) advise local authorities of ways in which administrative assistance and other support should be provided for councillors in their constituency role and as members of the executive; and

(d) illustrate ways of providing better quality information to councillors to assist them in their responsibilities as leaders of their communities, ward or divisional representatives, and as consumer champions.

Councillors' Allowances

4.14 In tandem with this, and to reinforce the means of achieving those objectives, we believe it is also necessary to make changes to the allowances system.

4.15 The current allowances system is described in Annex F. Critics of the current system make the following observations:

— the overall amount available for expenditure on allowances is inadequate; councillors are often subsidising the council;

— councillors with special responsibilities, for example the leader of the council or the chairs of committees, are not adequately compensated by the special responsibility allowance, given the maximum payment of £8,120;

— the allowances system is too heavily weighted in favour of attendance at formal meetings and discriminates against councillors who focus on group meetings or ward duties, and other important and valid activities;

— the interaction between the allowances system and the social security benefits system discriminates against unemployed people standing for election because they lose entitlement to claim unemployment benefit if, after taking into account reasonable expenses, they receive allowances of over £56 per week (which are intended only to cover their costs); and

— the withdrawal of the financial loss allowance (FLA) for councillors has acted as a disincentive to the self-employed standing for election.

4.16 These critics argue that the system discourages people from standing for election as councillors and from remaining as councillors for longer than one term of office. In particular it is said to discourage young people at the start of their careers, the self-employed, the unemployed, those in receipt of other benefits, and people with children and other dependent relatives. Several political groups told us that they found it increasingly difficult to recruit the right calibre of members willing to give up the time required to be a councillor.

4.17 The FLA was withdrawn by the Local Government and Housing Act 1989. It was thought then that it would be undesirable to have two alternative allowances available to councillors — the FLA or attendance allowance — when authorities were subject to an overall limit on the total they could spend on allowances. Also the overall uptake of FLA identified by Widdicombe was very low, on average only 3% of councillors in English shire counties, and 1% of all councillors. Nevertheless it has been represented to us that its removal has had a direct adverse effect on recruitment of councillors in certain areas and that it should be restored. We agree that its restoration should be considered. If it is restored it should be separately funded and not be a part of an authority's allowances scheme.

4.18 We believe there is little support for the creation of salaried councillors and we question the extent to which improvements to the allowance system will of themselves or alone make people more likely to stand for election or to stay on as councillors. We accept nevertheless that allowances have a part to play, and that the system should be amended to meet the objectives of ensuring that elected members do not suffer financial hardship and attracting a range of representative people to stand for election.

4.19 Therefore we recommend that, in order to that ensure people with a wide range of backgrounds are encouraged to serve as councillors, the Government should review, clarify and, as necessary, amend the allowances system to:

(a)   give local authorities greater discretion over what allowances to pay and to whom: there should be a substantial increase in the headroom within which each authority has the discretion to incur expenditure on allowances and the government should specify only a minimum basic allowance to be paid to all members;

(b)   remove the upper limit on the payment of special responsibility allowances;

(c)   make specified party meetings and single member duties eligible for payment of allowances;

(d)   require a report to be published on the operation of the scheme and on the level of payments to individual members;

(e)   review the interaction of the social security benefits' system and allowances' systems; and,

(f)   consider the restoration of the financial loss allowance for councillors.

Travel and Subsistence Allowances

4.20 The rate of travel allowances paid to officers is currently being renegotiated. Councillors and officers are paid different rates for travel and subsistence allowances and we believe this is unfair. We recommend that the Secretary of State should review the operation of the travel and subsistence allowances scheme for councillors in the light of the outcome of the negotiations of officers rates and align the levels of allowances paid to officers and councillors.

Other Support for Councillors

4.21 We have found there is considerable confusion about the extent to which local authorities can meet the costs of telephone rentals or bills, or other costs, such as child care costs, incurred by councillors in undertaking their duties. Some auditors have questioned long established practice quoting the basic allowance as being intended to cover these expenses. We believe that the position now needs to be clarified.

4.22 It is the view of the Department of the Environment and the local authority associations that child care costs and telephone call costs which are necessarily, and reasonably incurred in the course of, or to permit, the undertaking of duties as a councillor may be reimbursable by the local authority under the provisions of Section 111 of the Local Government Act 1972, subject to the Chief Finance Officer being satisfied that the money has been expended in the course of, or to permit, the undertaking of duties as a councillor.

4.23 We recommend that the Secretary of State issues a statement clarifying the extent to which he believes local authorities can meet the costs of services provided to members to permit them to carry out their duties as councillors, and considers the case for clarifying legislation as necessary.

4.24 From the evidence we have received it seems to be more often a shortage of time rather than of money which stops people from standing for election: employers are often reluctant to allow councillors more time off to perform their council duties than that which is statutorily required, and this is a particular deterrent for potential councillors at the beginning of their careers. One option which might merit studying could be a scheme which would permit the payment of councillor allowances directly to employers on condition that they made appropriate time off available to employees.

Statutory Committees

4.25 Currently local authorities are required to establish certain statutory committees — for example a Police Committee and a Social Services Committee. It has been put to us that in certain circumstances these requirements are unnecessarily prescriptive and have prevented authorities rationalising their internal management arrangements to provide more efficient and effective services.

4.26 We believe that the statutory requirement to establish such committees does impose unnecessary constraints on local authorities and inhibits experiments; and that to allow local authorities greater flexibility in the way they carry out functions in no way detracts from their importance. On the contrary, local authorities should be enabled to carry them out in the way they consider most appropriate.

Therefore we recommend to the Secretary of State that he considers, with his colleagues, whether or not, both as a part of possible experimental models discussed in Part V of this report and more generally, these statutory requirements should be lifted.

Part V

Is Further Change Necessary?

5.1 In this section we consider the case for making changes to the present statutory framework governing internal management which would permit more radical changes and experiments than can currently be undertaken. In response to our remit we provide examples of the kind of experimental executive models (paragraphs 5.11 to 5.78) which we believe would be suitable for trial by volunteering authorities The examples we give are only illustrations of the approaches we believe might be adopted and the impact we anticipate they would have on the operation of an authority. We are not recommending them for adoption by authorities. We would expect volunteering authories to devise schemes tailored to their own needs.

No Need for Change?

5.2 Many local authorities consider that the existing committee system is a satisfactory internal management mechanism. It is tried, tested, well established and understood by the public. It is sufficiently flexible to permit a multiplicity of arrangements to meet the needs and circumstances of individual authorities. It is open to the public and, in theory at least, allows for full debate by all council members, and therefore the proper scrutiny of the council's proposed actions or decisions. Councils therefore are openly accountable to the public for the decisions they take.

5.3 We agree that these are the major strengths of the committee system and any change must ensure that openness and accountability are preserved. But where decisions are taken outside the committee — and many decisions are taken in this way, by many authorities — these central objectives could, we believe, be achieved more efficiently and effectively by aligning appearance with reality.

Review of Overseas Models

5.4 In assessing the value of alternative internal management systems we considered a number of overseas models including those described in the consultation document. Some countries already operate an executive separate from the body of elected councillors and their experiences offer an insight into how these systems might work in England. But all the overseas systems which we have considered evolved from the existing framework of local government in those countries. We believe that any new systems for internal management in local authorities in England should similarly develop from what is already there , by a process of evolution. We do not support the wholesale adoption of overseas models in England simply because they are seen to work elsewhere. But they are important in so far as they help us question our own assumptions and suggest different approaches.

The Role of the Political Group and Political Leadership

5.5 The committee structure emerged and was developed at a time when local government was much less politicised than it is today. The growth of political organisation within local government has significantly altered the role of the councillor. The fact that in many authorities there is a majority party — which forms the administration — and a minority party or parties which form the opposition, challenges the pretence that all councillors have equal power and equal responsibilities. In practice they do not, and not only in majority councils.

5.6 Most major policy decisions in practice are taken not by the full council, its committees or sub-committees but elsewhere within the ruling group — where there is a majority group — or in consultation with the leadership of other groups where there is a minority administration or coalition. The majority party, where there is one, through its lead members and especially its leader, is a de facto executive, given authority by the party group. Formal authority may rest with the full council, or with the committee, but the real authority rests with individuals and not with the committee or council structure.

5.7 The Local Government and Housing Act 1989 obliges authorities to proceed as if the formal position were the reality. Decisions already taken by the de facto executive have to be reconsidered and taken again within the formal committee system.

5.8 We believe that this inconsistency between existing prcatice and the internal management arrangements described in the legislation and accompanying regulations is inherently unsatisfactory and prevents clear accountability. Nevertheless we accept that the risks of abuse which gave rise to the 1989 Act remain. And in deference to our remit we have not pursued the possibility of wholesale replacement of the 1989 Act regime for all authorities.

5.9 Nevertheless of all the representations made to us by local authorities the most consistent one was that there should be limited legislative change which would permit formal deliberative committees without executive powers, outside the terms of the 1989 Act. We describe below the possible form and likely effect of a single party committee which we believe would be acceptable as part of an experiment by a volunteering authority. After monitoring this aspect of any experiments the Government and the local authority Associations may well want to consider the desirability of replacing the 1989 Act provisions on political balance in deliberative committees with a more permissive regime for all authorities.

5.10 The example we give below can apply where there is a single party advisory committee. But this will not always be the case. In authorities where no single party has overall control two or more parties may wish to form a coalition and themselves enjoy the advantages an advisory committee can provide, excluding other party groups from membership. In those circumstances the same or similar considerations and safeguards which we describe below would apply. This would also be true in the case of the examples of executive models which we describe on pages 44-51 below.

The Single Party Advisory Committee

5.11 The committee could, by definition, make recommendations only and not take executive decisions. It would probably consist of the leader, deputy leader and committee chairmen and women of the majority party. But others may be included.

5.12 The committee would probably not meet in public, unless it chose to, and would therefore be able to receive the advice of officers in a confidential setting. Its deliberations should result in clearer policy guidance and recommendations being issued to executive committees. Such a system would also clarify the source of recommendations being put to committees — no longer requiring officers, unless it was professionally desirable for them to do so, to put forward a range of officer recommendations — and would therefore enhance accountability both to the council and to the public.

Role of the Council

5.13 Council and member roles would be little changed. The current workings of the political policy making machine would merely be brought into the formal structure of the council. Committees would continue to consider, and may reject, the recommendations of the advisory committee subject only to the usual political pressures. But members would benefit from having identified people to hold to account for the policy recommendations they consider.

Role of officers

5.14 Currently officers can and do advise single party groups on policy issues but this has to be done on an informal basis. Many officers would like to see this process formalised and brought out into the open. We agree with them that this is likely to reduce the potential for the politicisation of the officer cadre and would also ensure that policies were developed and determined on the basis of the best possible advice. The relationship between the officers and other members would remain unchanged.

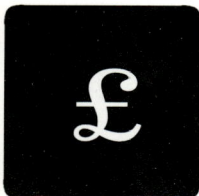

Allowances

5.15 Recognition of the single party policy committee is often a matter only of formalising existing practice. Therefore it would not require any greater time commitment from members, whether leaders or backbenchers. We hope that the allowances system will permit payment of attendance allowances for single party meetings, in line with our recommendations at paragraph 4.19 (c).

Safeguards

5.16 Currently, since the single party advisory committee has no official status, members have no rights of access to papers produced for it or by it. If the advisory committee is formally recognised there will be a statutory requirement for its papers to be made public. But as a deliberative forum it is unnecessary to require the advisory committee to publish a record of its deliberations or the papers it commissions in the early stages of policy development, provided that its recommendations are public. Members have statutory rights of access to papers and rights at common law which give them a prima facie right to inspect documents addressed to the council of which they are a member. It would be necessary to restrict these rights if the single party committee's confidentiality was to be preserved.

5.17 As a quid pro quo, it might be necessary to require an advisory committee to publish accounts of the reasoning behind its recommendations. The general principle, that authorities should have regard only to proper matters and should have in mind all such matters at the time they take decisions — and be able to demonstrate this — will continue to apply. All facts which go before an advisory committee must be capable of being exposed more widely within the council.

Legal position

5.18 To permit these changes it would be necessary to remove the stipulation under section 15 of the Local Government and Housing Act 1989 that committees should be politically balanced and that every committee should have at least two political groups represented on it. It would also be necessary to prescribe standing orders to require that a committee formed on this basis could only make recommendations, not take decisions. The Local Government (Access to Information Act) 1985 would need to be amended to disapply it to such deliberative committees.

Political Executives

5.19 Because the present legislative framework excludes the political group from a formal place in the decision-making process it prevents its development into a distinct body. But the party group plays an important part in the formulation of policy and issues will continue to be discussed at its meetings whatever internal management arrangements are put in place.

5.20 In many authorities, most major policy decision making takes place initially within the political group process and only afterwards is validated by the formal committee system. It is common in authorities with a controlling majority group for an inner grouping of the wider political group to have developed into an informal quasi-executive, or cabinet.

5.21 The position would be clarified by legislation to allow the non-executive advisory committee, described above, to be put in place. But there is also scope for developing such one party advisory committees, or one or more party advisory committees where there isn't majority control, into executive models.

Advantages of the Executive Model

5.22 The advantages claimed for such executive models include that they provide clear political direction for the authority; make clear where accountability lies; provide a more efficient, quicker and co-ordinated decision making process; and provide a confidential forum for the ruling group to test the range of policy options with its official advisers.

Possible Models

5.23 We have identified four broad categories into which executive models might fit. They are as follows:

❖ a directly elected single person executive

❖ a directly elected multi-person executive

❖ a single person executive appointed from the council

❖ a multi-person executive appointed from the council.

5.24 These categories all envisage an executive which would consist of politicians. There is also an option for a single person executive officer — the council manager model — who would have delegated executive powers but would remain an employee of the authority. This option was included in the consultation paper but received little support. Accordingly we do not discuss it here but concentrate on models where the executive consists of elected representatives. Nevertheless we would not discourage authorities from considering the council manager model.

5.25 Options (a) and (b) above would provide a mandate either to an individual in the form of a mayor or to multi-person directly elected executive. Either option risks a difficult and unclear relationship between those mandated and the separately elected council, particularly where the executive, either singular or plural, does not command a majority in the council. Options (c) and (d) in which the executive is drawn from the body of the council would normally overcome such structural conflicts. The responses to the consultation paper showed little or no enthusiasm for a mayoral system, whether by election or appointment. We have discovered only marginal support for options (a) and (b) and we believe they are impractical at the moment, although we would not discourage authorities from thinking about them. Here, we have decided to concentrate attention on the implications of a multi-person executive drawn from the council membership. And within this basic model we have identified two broad models:

(1) an executive drawn from the council which has collective responsibility for the whole range of functions delegated to it; and

(2) an executive drawn from the council which similarly has collective responsibility for the functions delegated to it but with specific portfolios allocated to individual members of the executive. Individual portfolios could follow traditional service lines or could be based on functional responsibilities, geographical splits or other criteria.

5.26 We have rejected models including an executive made up in part of unelected people co-opted from outside, because we do not believe it is acceptable to include on the executive people who do not have direct accountability to their electorate. But this need not prevent the executive getting advice from experts whenever they felt it was desirable to do so.

5.27 There is not one simple or straightforward model which would fit each of these broad categories. We believe there is a continuum along which there is a range of executive models which can evolve one from the other, sharing some, but not all, characteristics. Paragraphs 5.11 to 5.18 describe the single party advisory committee. Paragraphs 5.41 to 5.78 describe four other examples of possible models.

The Role of the Executive

5.28 In all our executive models we would expect the executive to take responsibility for strategic decisions of the authority. It would also take all major policy decisions within an approved budget with the scope of these being defined in advance. These executive responsibilities could be allocated:

— to the executive collectively — this system would have implications for the development of specialisation in members; reporting arrangements for officers; and defining accountability;

— to individual members of the executive on the basis of some sort of portfolio; this would need careful definition of the extent of delegation from the executive within that portfolio; and a description of the issues which would be reserved to the executive as a whole.

5.29 These allocations of responsibilities to, and within, the executive could be applied to the whole range of possible models.

Confidentiality

5.30 For the executive to secure the benefits of frank discussion of policy options, it would need to be able to call for papers and hold discussions with official advisers outside the scope of the present freedom of information legislation. If this were permitted clear instructions would be required on how information was to be provided to the rest of the council.

The Role of the Officer

5.31 The introduction of a separate executive will in certain models have implications for the officers of an authority, who presently are responsible to the council as a whole and employed by it.

5.32 Chief officers and most departmental staff would become responsible to an executive, rather than to the full council — even though they would still be employed by the latter. It would then be necessary to consider how advice and support were provided to the council (and its scrutiny committees, if they were formed) and to individual councillors. To make arrangements effective it may be necessary to form a separate officer support group for councillors not on the executive. This could be done by staff having well defined responsibilities or by secondment arrangements. Equally it could be through the development of a separate, but probably relatively small, cadre of staff to support any scrutiny process.

5.33 The issue is acutely focused in the role of the chief executive who will need to act as a cabinet secretary to the executive; as chief executive in carrying out the executive policy; and as chief officer to the council. Again, carefully defined responsibilities might be the solution, but equally there could be the appointment of a separate clerk to the council who would act as a monitoring officer and see that the council's rights of scrutiny were protected.

The Scrutiny Role: Overseeing the Executive

5.34 The transfer of significant responsibility to an executive would only be acceptable if coupled with clear and systematic procedures for the rest of the council to oversee and scrutinise its activities. It would be necessary to strike a balance between the benefits to be gained from a more efficient decision-making process and the ability of the council as a whole to influence the executive's policy and actions. A distinction would need to be made between opportunities for scrutiny when councillors would be able to influence the policy before decisions are taken, and later scrutiny of the effectiveness of policy decisions — where they could assess the implications of past decisions and the quality of services being provided. An authority proposing an executive model would need to specify the extent to which certain issues within the responsibilities of the executive would need to be subject to prior scrutiny by the wider council. This prior scrutiny would take place in a number of fora, but typically would be triggered by requiring a proposal to be published before it becomes final, allowing discussion by all councillors as well as others.

5.35 The scrutiny role is carried out by a variety of people within and outside the authority. Inside the authority, these would be the council as a whole and individual councillors, scrutiny or select committees, and the monitoring officer. Outside the authority scrutiny is provided by statutory inspectorates; external auditors; the local government ombudsman; and informal scrutiny operates via pressure groups and public opinion.

5.36 For there to be an adequate counterbalance to the creation of a seperate executive, any committee or scrutiny panel established to examine its policies, decisions or actions would need to have clear rights, including:

— prior scrutiny of certain categories of executive proposals;

— scrutiny of decisions after they are taken;

— the right to chose areas of scrutiny;

— the right to question executive members, and officials;

— access to officers' advice and technical support; and

— access to the inspectorates, including auditors.

The Representative Role

5.37 A principal virtue of the executive model is that councillors, free from routine and time consuming involvement in traditional decision-making committees, will in addition to their role in the scrutiny of the executive be able to develop their role as representatives and leaders of their communities.

5.38 As in the scrutiny role, an important element in the success of a councillor's role in constituency work will be the extent to which the authority will provide officer advice and technical support. Members would require access to professional advice to assist judgements on the effectiveness of policies and also data on their local impact to allow them to monitor quality in the delivery of services. This will have implications for the role of local government officers, as already mentioned.

Decentralisation

5.39 The community leadership role as well as the authority's day to day operations could be further enhanced by some degree of devolution of powers to area or neighbourhood committees. In these circumstances there are opportunities for local people to determine their own priorities about the level and quality of services they receive. It would also provide an opportunity for councillors to become consumer champions monitoring and reviewing not only the services provided by their authority but by other public and private agencies.

The Rights of Minority Groups

5.40 The position of councillors from minority parties is obviously affected by the rights given to councillors generally in the scrutiny process, but there are some issues peculiar to opposition groups. In a system of scrutiny committees, opposition members could hold some or all chairs; or be given equality of membership on scrutiny committees, and/or they could be given the right to choose areas of investigation. Minority groups should be able to secure debates on the issues of their choice at the full council meeting and there also need to be agreed procedures for recording and reporting decisions of the executive to councillors generally. Clearer guidelines on the provision of papers to all councillors would need to be provided and similar safeguards to those described in 5.16 and 5.17 above would need to be introduced.

Political Executives: Some Examples

5.41 We are not proposing that any of the examples of executive models described below should be adopted by volunteering authorities nor do we claim to have identified all of the various parts of each model. We seek to illustrate possible models and a range of their possible consequences. They should be helpful as a start to debate and as a reference point in devising possible approaches.

5.42 Each of the examples given below assumes that our recommendations on changes to the allowances system (at paragraphs 4.19 to 4.23) have been accepted. The key features of each example are illustrated in Table 1, page 52 . The effects they would have on the role of members are illustrated in Figure 1, page 53.

Example 1: The Single Party Executive Committee

5.43 In this example the council delegates to the single party policy committee a limited range of executive powers and formulation of a broad strategy. Decisions taken by the executive would become decisions of the council. The precise extent of the executive's control over policy would be at the discretion of the council and would be laid out in Standing Orders. Authorities could retain certain functions either with the full council or with other specialist committees — for example approving the budget, and planning decisions. The executive would retain only an advisory role in such matters. The policy executive would set the broad strategic framework within which day to day matters were dealt with by the service committees or officers and have a right to call in committee and officer decisions. Its decisions could be challenged and or vetoed by the full council. Standing Orders would prescribe the circumstances in which recall and veto could take place, and the mechanisms for doing so.

Role of the Council

5.44 The executive cannot work in isolation in this model and all councillors, majority and minority, will need to be provided with opportunities for more rigorous scrutiny of policy formulation so that they may have a direct effect on the determination of provision and standards before decisions are implemented. This would also need to be backed up by performance review panels to fine-tune policy in operation and to ensure that service standards and targets were met.

Role of officers

5.45 Officers would have to serve both the executive, in the formulation of policy, and the councillors who scrutinised and reviewed such policy. Some officers might feel compromised by this, particularly if they have to assist in the scrutiny of areas of policy where they had taken a part in policy formulation. But such difficulties seem superable. Members of the review panels or scrutiny committees might also seek independent expert advice from people such as the external auditor.

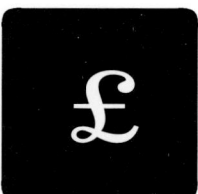

Allowances

5.46 It would be necessary to enhance the Special Responsibility Allowances (SRA) and/or provide salaries which would be available for members of the policy executive to reflect the level of responsibilities they take on. The basic allowance would be paid to all councillors together with allowances for specified single duties.

Safeguards

5.47 Leading members in deciding whether or not to recommend this example would have to balance the advantages of the current system — where they can have the benefit of receiving officers' advice in an informal setting without the scrutiny of other members — with the advantages of being provided with executive powers, but being subject to closer scrutiny by other councillors. Officers would need to ensure that non-executive members had adequate access to information. As in the single party advisory committee there will be circumstances in which the executive wishes to keep its deliberations secret but the reasoning behind its recommendations or decisions will need to be made public. The same changes to legislation restricting access to information would therefore be required, as at paragraph 5.18…

5.48 It would be necessary to prescribe in standing orders rules covering:

(a) the disclosure of reasoning behind recommendations or decisions by the executive;

(b) the circumstances in which decisions of the executive may be called in and overturned;

(c) the procedures for replacing members and/or the whole executive;

(d) arrangements for calling members of the executive before council or committees of the council to explain their actions; and

(e) the extent of delegation from the council to the executive and from the executive to committees and officers.

Legal Position

5.49 Similar legislative changes would be required as for the single party advisory committee.

Example 2:   The Lead Member System

5.50 In this example the council delegates executive powers to named lead members rather than to a collective political executive. For example the council would delegate control over social service decisions to the chair of the Social Services Committee. Lead members could form themselves into a non-executive committee and its members would now have individual executive powers to carry out the policies agreed in their meetings.

5.51 The committee system could still operate but they would be used for scrutiny rather than executive purposes. However the extent of committees' powers would vary. To produce speedier, more accountable, and more business-like decision taking, the following order of precedence seems most likely to be adopted:

❖ **Full council**

❖ **Lead member**

❖ **Committee and sub-committee**

❖ **Officer**

The Role of the Council

5.52 In such a scheme the lead member would be free to take decisions but would be accountable to the full council. Service committee members would still be involved in the determination of standards and provisions but they would become more concerned with offering advice to the lead member and scrutinising their decisions and actions.

5.53 Some decisions will be delegated to lead members and some to officers. The committee would not be able to overturn the decisions of the lead member but it would have powers to refer contentious decisions to the full council for approval. This would require a system of notification of all lead member decisions to committee members before implementation and a process of calling these decisions in if a set proportion of members wished the decision to be debated and approved by full council.

5.54 It would not be as necessary to establish separate scrutiny committees, or review panels, as envisaged under example one because the service committees could continue to perform this function. But they remain an additional option.

5.55 It may be necessary to prescribe in Standing Orders certain committees which should be excluded from this regime. For example, it seems inappropriate to delegate to a single member responsibility for planning decisions.

Role of Officers

5.56 At present the officer is the only individual to whom decision-taking powers may be delegated. If this right is extended to a member there is a risk that member/officer relationships may become more confrontational. It will therefore be necessary to specify that the ultimate power in deciding how to implement the council's policies lies with the member. To safeguard the officer's professional status and neutrality, officers may need to be provided with an opportunity to put their advice or contrary view to the council, or at least to a council committee.

5.57 It ought not, in our view, to be necessary to create a twin-track officer structure with one branch serving the lead members and another the rest of the council.

Allowances

5.58 It would be necessary to enhance the SRA, or pay a salary to lead members to reflect the extra burdens they took on. They should also receive appropriate administrative support, and training especially in technical areas of responsibility.

Safeguards

5.59 Lead members will require adequate information to take decisions and they are likely to have greater access to information than their committee members. Therefore it will be necessary for officers to ensure that the substantive information behind any lead member's decision is made available to the committee. What constituted such information would be the decision of the officer and not the lead member.

5.60 Most of the necessary safeguards to ensure the probity and accountability of the lead member system are already in operation and may be adapted from the current system. Standing orders will be important in setting the framework within which decisions can be taken and the circumstances under which they should be reviewed. Also it will be necessary to provide for the removal of lead members in certain, specified, circumstances.

Legal Position

5.61 It will be necessary to extend section 101 of Local Government Act 1972 to permit the delegation of the discharge of council functions to individual members. The rest of the current statutory framework will remain in place. More important will be the local authority's standing orders. They will need to prescribe, as a minimum, the powers delegated to each lead member, the process of notification and calling in lead members decisions for further review, the extent of officer support provided to the lead member, and the process by which lead members are appointed and removed.

Example 3:   The Cabinet System

5.62 This example extends the principle of delegation to lead members to include a single party policy committee the membership of which has individual and combined executive powers. It is imprecisely referred to as the cabinet system, and we use that term here only as a form of useful shorthand. Much of what was outlined under models one and two would also apply in this example.

5.63 Decisions taken by the executive would be decisions of the council. Individual members of the executive would have delegated areas of responsibility, and the attendant decision-taking powers; but the broader strategy would be decided by the executive. It would be necessary to specify in standing orders the division of responsibilities between the council and the executive and the executive and individual members of the executive. Standing orders would lay down the circumstances under which the council could overturn the executive's decisions, and the executive could overturn a lead member's decision.

5.64 It will be necessary to provide a system for informing the executive of decisions taken by a lead member without prior consultation. This will generally involve day-to-day operational matters because lead members will not usually be allowed to take strategic decisions without executive approval. The cabinet would also be the forum in which disputes between lead members or departments were settled.

5.65 The cabinet would determine the strategic framework for the authority and identify its operational goals.

Role of the Council

5.66 The full council will have the power to overturn at least some decisions taken by the executive or lead members. It will be for the council to decide how much of its executive power it wishes to retain. As a minimum we would expect this to cover the setting of the budget — based on recommendations from the executive. The council will also require regular reports on the decisions taken by the executive and its lead members; these might be provided by a separate secretariat.

5.67 The executive role of the current committee structure will inevitably be weakened as more power is vested in the committee chairs and the executive, and as the executive takes on the role of overseeing and scrutinizing the lead members' actions.

5.68 The council will scrutinize policy formulation and implementation through a committee structure. Their involvement in policy formulation will maintain the input of all councillors into the strategic approach being adopted by the council. The committee structure is likely to vary but at its heart will be scrutiny. Committees with a scrutiny function will need to have rights, and possibly membership which has a balance in favour of the minority parties. This could be done by allocating memberships disproportionately from that on the full council or by giving chairmanships to minority party members.

Role of Officers

5.69 The cabinet system raises questions about the career structures of officers. Under this system a separate secretariat could be established to service the executive, and if scrutiny committees were established, a secretariat might be necessary to service them. Officers who were members of the secretariat could be drawn from the council staff and not be employees of the executive. A dual career structure ought not therefore to be necessary.

Safeguards

5.70 Standing Orders would need to prescribe the division of responsibility between the council and executive and between the executive and the lead members. Mechanisms would need to be put in place to keep the council informed of the decisions of the executive and the executive of decisions of lead members and their committees. Standing Orders would also be needed to specify systems of recall and requisition.

Legal Position

5.71 The legislative changes outlined in paras 5.18 and 5.61 would also be necessary in this Model.

Example 4: The Strong Political Executive — Separate Legal Entity

5.72 In this example there would be a separate executive with its own legal powers and status. It would take control of the decision taking process on behalf of the council. Its membership would be drawn entirely from the council membership. It would not need to be politically balanced and minority party input into the formulation of policy would be discretionary. The executive would decide how to apportion powers, ie whether to adopt individual and/or collective responsibility.

5.73 Under the most extreme version of this example the executive would take over all the decision taking powers currently with the full council. It would then be for the executive to decide to what extent it would delegate powers back to the full council, to committees, or to officers. It would be necessary to determine in advance the extent of the powers to be given to the full council to overturn the decisions of the executive. Standing orders could be used to develop a call-in system and/or allow for the dismissal of the executive. It would be necessary to decide whether or not the final say over certain decisions, for example approving the budget, would stay with the full council.

Role of the Council

5.74 The role for councillors not on this strong executive would need to be strengthened by developing their representative and consumer champion roles. Their scrutiny and constituency roles would need to be promoted in similar ways to those described in other examples and structural changes could be introduced to decentralise operational decisions to neighbourhood or area committees and devolve substantial responsibilities to them. Non-executive members would be members and chair these committees.

5.75 The committees would be fora for considering the strategic decisions of the executive but would also review service provision in their area — as consumer watchdogs they would review all service provision not only that of the authority. Their budgets would be set by the executive.

Role of Officers

5.76 Because of the separation of powers envisaged in this example officers serving the executive would be under a separate contract of employment from those serving the council. It will be necessary to define the working relationship between the two groups of officers as between the executive and the council. The executive would take officer advice and set its own level of delegation to them, as would the council. We would expect there to be two separate career structures.

Safeguards

5.77 The extent to which safeguards can be imposed on this model will depend upon the degree of autonomy vested in the executive. The most important safeguard, the reversal of executive decisions by the council, would not be available other than for the setting of the budget.

Legal Position

5.78 Comprehensive legislation would be necessary to provide the executive with a separate legal identity from the council.

Table 1

KEY FEATURES OF THE FOUR EXAMPLES OF EXECUTIVE MODELS

Model	Single Party Executive Committee	Lead Member System	Cabinet System	Executive As Separate Entity
Attribute	Example 1	Example 2	Example 3	Example 4
Formal single party executive committee	yes	no but lead members 'advise'	yes	yes
Delegation to individual members	no	yes specified extensive areas only	yes specified limited areas only	executive discretion
Ultimate decision taking body	full council	full council	full council	executive (limited powers reserved to full council)
Possible changes to the allowances system	—	lead member and chief officer meetings eligible for allowances	possibly salaried full time leader of council	members on executive to be salaried and full time
Role of officers	employed by council dual role in policy formulation and review	employed by council	employed by council dual role in policy formulation and review	employed by council with possible separate employment contracts with executive
Opportunities for members generally	more time for representative role and scrutiny role enhanced			
Access to information	because of the requirement for confidentiality there will be a reduction in access to information which will be offset by improved provision by officers of ward based and other information			
Extent of committee powers under each example	powers delegated by executive	policy committees subordinate to lead members	less influence	scrutiny role some power delegated by executive

Figure 1
THE CHANGING ROLE OF MEMBERS UNDER AN EXECUTIVE MODEL

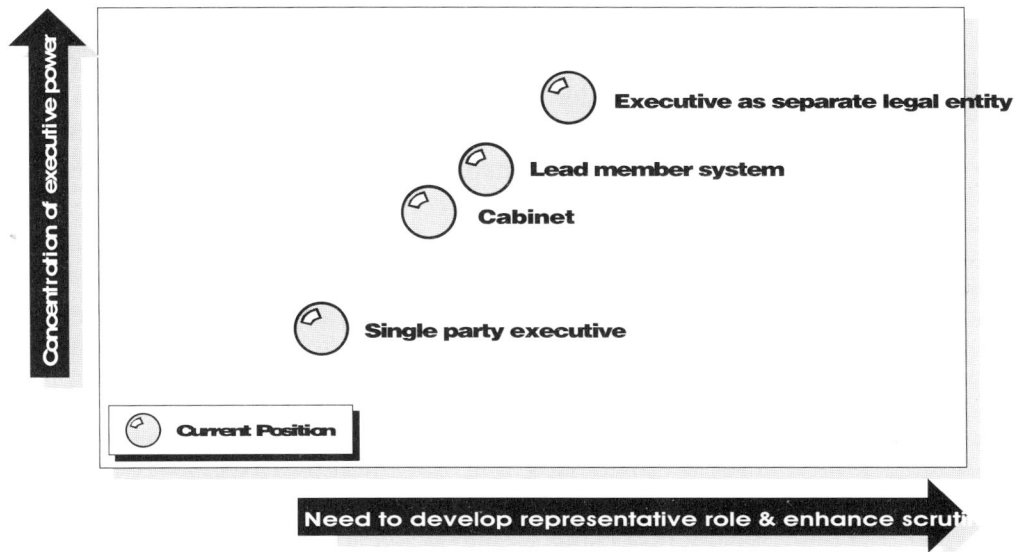

The graph shows the correlation between the concentration of executive power in the hands of a few members and the extent to which the need to enhance members' representative and scrutiny roles becomes more important.

Conclusion

5.79 The range of executive models of political management that we have described are aimed at streamlining policy development and decision-making at council level. As more powers are given to some councillors, the role of all others will change. And in our report we have underlined the corresponding importance of developing the scrutiny and representative role of councillors. We have also sought to underline the case for experimentation to support the role of local councillors in leading and representing their local communities. Some of the councils we have visited have developed extensive systems of delegation through neighbourhood and area committees to promote these roles. Others have developed partnerships between local councillors and their town and parish councils in both consultative and advisory capacities. To the extent that these developments are constrained or inhibited by existing legislation, there is scope for authorities to come forward with proposals for experimentation either within or outside any ideas they might have on developing a political executive.

5.80 We are not arguing that any authority should be obliged to change its existing internal management arrangements to fit in with the examples given above. We are not proposing a strait-jacket approach. Our aim has been to look at the various things that are being done by local authorities and to examine the scope for and the implications of removing obstacles which prevent them being done better still.

5.81 To test the effect and desirability of removing those obstacles we recommend that the Secretary of State for the Environment should take powers to allow, in consultation with local government, experimental changes to their internal management arrangements proposed by individual local authorities. Legislation would allow approval of experiments including the following ingredients, amongst others, subject to suitable safeguards:

(a) the replacing of the existing committee structure and the introduction of executive models and other structures of political management,

(b) the creation of deliberative committees whose membership consisted only of members of the majority group (or dominant coalition group),

(c) the decentralisation of decision-taking,

(d) new rights for councillors to review and scrutinise council decisions, and

(e) enhanced roles for councillors not in executive positions.

We hope this report will encourage a debate and search for more effective ways of decision making, organising council business and improving accountability.

Part VI

Suggested Approach for Authorisation of Experimental Schemes

6.1 At 2.11 we have recorded our recommendations. Where they relate to the promotion of good practice some will require minor legislative changes or amending regulations. But our recommendations to permit experimental models will require primary legislation and the putting into place of mechanisms for the assessment and review of proposals put forward by volunteering authorities.

6.2 In this section of the report we suggest the key points which would need to be addressed and the form those mechanisms might take.

Approval of Experimental Models

6.3 Authorities which decide to experiment with internal management arrangements not possible under the existing statutory framework would be required to present a scheme to the Secretary of State describing the model they intended to use, specifying its effects and outlining any safeguards which in their view it would be necessary to introduce. We would expect each proposal as a minimum to:-

— set out the background to the authority's decision to experiment, i.e provide an explanation of how the current statute restricts further development of the authority's internal management arrangements;

— provide a brief description of the changes being proposed, concentrating on the areas where freedom from current legislative restrictions was being sought;

— itemise the objectives of any plan, its appropriateness to local circumstances, and explain how the benefits were to be monitored;

— describe the effect it was anticipated the proposal would have on the relationship between officers and members and their respective roles; describe the safeguards which would be put in place, and the roles of the minority and majority parties;

55

— list the revised standing orders which the authority would be required to adopt to regulate the new system, e.g defining the relationship between the executive and full council; and

— propose the period of time the authority expected the experiment to run and set out any contingency arrangement the authority thought it would be necessary to put in place, including what would happen in the event of a change in political control and the circumstances under which the experiment may be cancelled: the length of individual experiments would vary but we would not expect them to be established for a period shorter than one electoral cycle.

Mechanism for Approval

6.4   We recommend that for this purpose the Secretary of State should appoint a panel of advisers to consider applications put to him for consent to establish an experimental model; membership of the panel should include nominees from DOE, from the local authority associations the Audit Commission, and The Local Government Management Board.

6.5   The panel would consider all applications by local authorities. Where it found their proposals unacceptable, because they did not meet terms of reference which the panel would publish, for example because it failed on grounds of probity or fairness to minority groups, it would suggest amendments and modifications. The panel would then recommend acceptance or rejection.

Monitoring of Experimental Models

6.6   In view of the unknown nature and possible effects of the experiments we also recommend that where experimental models are approved they should be subject to annual review by the advisory panel which should publish annual reports. The Secretary of State should have powers to suspend or modify an experimental model or models where the panel reported they were failing; and after a period of time to be determined the panel should evaluate the experimental models and make appropriate recommendations to the Secretary of State about their possible wider application in authorities which wished to adopt them, or their continuation without time limit if the experimenting authority so wished.

Annex A ────────────────

Membership of the Working Party

The membership of the Working Party was as follows:

Association of Metropolitan Authorities

Rodney Brooke, Secretary
Terry Hanafin, Chief Executive, London Borough of Lewisham
Ben Clayden

Association of County Councils

Robin Wendt, Secretary
Ian Caulfield, Chief Executive, Warwickshire County Council
Roy Williams

Association of District Councils

Geoffrey Filkin, Secretary
Mel Usher, Chief Executive, South Somerset District Council
John Rees, Legal Under Secretary
Andrew Purssell

The Local Government Management Board

Michael Clarke, Chief Executive

The Audit Commission

Peter Brokenshire, Acting Controller (June 1992 to January 1993)
Bob Chilton, Director of Local Government Studies (January 1993 —)

The London School of Economics and Political Science

Professor George Jones, Professor of Government, London School of Economics and Politics

The Department of the Environment

The Working Party was Chaired by the Department of the Environment which also provided the Secretariat. Its representatives were:

Robin Young, (Chairman)
Lindsay Bell
Steven Watts (Secretary)
Paul Garwood

Annex B————————————————————————————

Consultation Paper Proposals

B.1 In this section we summarise the consultation paper *The Internal Management of Local Authorities in England* which was published by the Department of the Environment in July 1991, and the responses to it.

General Background

B.2 In publishing the consultation paper the Government recognised that there were a wide range of possible improvements which could be adopted, and that different approaches would be appropriate in different areas. It also acknowledged that change might not be appropriate for all authorities.

B.3 The Government's view was that the objectives of any change in management arrangements should be to:

— promote more effective, speedy and business-like decision making;

— enhance the scrutiny of decisions;

— increase the interest taken by the public in the local government; and

— provide scope for councillors to devote more time to their constituency role

It also recognised that checks and balances against abuse of power by majority parties -particularly in areas where political control very rarely changes hands — must remain important considerations.

Options for the Future

B.4 The consultation paper did not present an exhaustive list of all the possible options but provided a brief description of the principal models:

(1)   the retention of the present system of Internal Management;

(2)   adaptation of the committee system, which might involve changes to the legislative framework to allow councils to delegate decision-making to

committee chairmen or might involve reconsideration of the need for minority representation on committees;

(3)   the introduction of a cabinet system, with powers delegated to committee chairmen or to an executive of elected members chosen from the council as a whole;

(4)   a council manager who would be appointed by the council to take over the day-to-day running of the authority;

(5)   a directly elected executive, with separate elections to the council and to the executive; and

(6)   a directly elected mayor.

B.5   The consultation paper invited comments on the remuneration and administrative support for councillors; the need to safeguard the political neutrality of officers; the numbers of councillors; electoral arrangements; and the need to review existing safeguards and access to information.

Responses to the Consultation Paper

B.6   Over 600 responses were received, of which 245 favoured leaving the present internal management arrangements unchanged. The following table shows the numbers of respondents who favoured the options outlined in the consultation paper:

	All	Principal Local Authorities*
Adaptation of committee system	53	39
Cabinet system	27	10
Council manager	16	8
Directly elected executive	5	0
Directly elected mayor	4	0
Remuneration for some councillors	16	8
Remuneration for all councillors	33	21

County Councils, Shire and Metropolitan Districts and London Boroughs

B.7   Particularly amongst local authority respondents the more radical the proposition the lower was the level of support. The greatest support was for systems which built on existing structures and precedents.

B.8 Respondents proposed other changes to the committee system, including the relaxation of the regulations governing substitution on committees; and the removal of the requirement to establish certain committees — such as education and social services.

B.9 Those who supported the adoption of the cabinet system mostly envisaged an executive formed by committee chairmen. A number of authorities felt that they had already established some form of 'cabinet' system albeit on an informal basis. They supported legislation to permit single-party committees in order to legitimise what was already being done in practice.

B.10 Concern was expressed that a cabinet system would concentrate power in fewer hands, alter the nature of accountability, and diminish the role of non-executive council members, echoing the dissent the Maud report in 1967. There was concern too that the rights of minority parties might be adversely affected, and that safeguards would need to be put in place to ensure that this did not occur.

B.11 Although it received only limited support, the proposal to appoint an officer as council manager to take over the day-to-day running of the authority was thought to be worthy of further investigation.

B.12 Very little support was expressed for a directly elected executive or a directly elected mayor — and no support for either option was received from principal authorities. The main objections were that there would be conflict and confused accountability between the elected executive or mayor and the full council. It was argued that this option would undesirably reduce the role of elected councillors and that it would be difficult to ensure the political neutrality of officers with two masters. Its advocates argued that a directly elected executive or mayor would revive local government as a democratic force; and would allow the council to play its proper role in scrutinising executive decisions.

Councillor's Remuneration

B.13 There was no consensus on whether councillors should be salaried or receive allowances, but most respondents fet that the principle of voluntary service should be retained. Many wanted to see a greater degree of discretion given to authorities in the allocation of allowances according to local circumstances. Some saw the current system as a positive disincentive to the retention or the recruitment of councillors. Proponents of the cabinet system supported enhanced allowances for those councillors who were members of an executive, but that this would only be workable if the resources made available for the payment of allowances was increased.

B.14 There was widespread support for the provision of additional secretarial and administrative support for councillors.

Numbers of Councillors

B.15 The majority of respondents agreed that the proper number of councillors on each council should be considered on a case by case basis. Many thought it inappropriate to propose changes before the outcome of deliberations of the Local Government Commission. If an executive model was adopted it would be necessary to consider what were the appropriate number of councillors to fulfil the scrutinising and the representative roles.

Access to Information

B.16 Respondents supported the view that there should be no further restriction on the access to information which councillors enjoyed. However they acknowledged that certain models would necessarily affect access rights — the elected executive, or the single — party committee. The predominant view was that safeguards would need to be introduced to ensure that councillors had access to appropriate material.

Annex C———————————————————

Task Force — Questionnaire

A General

(i) What are the main problems faced in the internal management of local authorities?

(ii) How should they be resolved?

(iii) What legislative changes would be required?

(iv) General topics to be covered:

(a) the Committee system

(b) political leadership

(c) the role of the Councillor

(d) Councillor/Officer relationships and the position of the Chief Executive.

B Delegation of Powers

(i) What is the Council's current practice for delegating decisions?

(ii) Did the councils practice of delegation change following the Hillingdon judgement?

(iii) How is emergency business dealt with between Committees?

(iv) Is effective management of the Council inhibited by the restrictions placed on delegation to individual members?

(v)   Would delegation of decision making only to the Chairman of Committees improve the situation? How?

(vi)   Should there be wider delegation to:

    (a)   members (sub-committees and individuals)?

    (b)   Officers?

(vii)   With the increasing numbers of partnerships (City Challenge etc) should there be delegation to Committees with outside membership? Should those outside members be able to vote?

(viii) Should there be delegation to companies?

(ix)   What would be the effects of delegating decision making to Neighbourhood Committees? In some cases all the ward members representing a Neighbourhood are from the same political party. How would minority groups views be represented?

C   Executive of Elected Members

(i)   Is there a recognised leadership group? What is its relationship with the officer structure? Does it act as an unofficial political executive? Has the position changed as a result of the Widdicombe legislation? Did that cause problems?

(ii)   Does the leadership group operate effectively within the current legislation?

(iii)   How could its operation be improved by changes to legislation?

(iv)   Should changes to legislation accommodate the need to allow party groups to operate within the formal committee structure of the authority? For example an executive committee made up of a Chairman or Chairwomen of the Committee all of whom are appointed by the majority party. Or some other form of executive. Should the leadership group have executive powers, and if so which, and what impact would this have on the Committees?

(v)   What would need to be done to safeguard:

    (a)   the rights of minority parties?

    (b)   the rights of backbenchers?

    (c)   the political neutrality officers?

(vi) Where an executive of elected members is drawn from one political party would access to information need to be restricted to other councillors and to the public? If so, how?

(vii) In the case of hung councils: Is there a leadership group, what form does it take. How could it be improved?

(viii) How would this model work in an independently run Council?

D   Strategic Management

(i) What arrangements has the authority for broad strategic management ie. methods through which the authority reviews the outside of the environment, assesses key tasks, determines priorities, reviews performance and then evaluates organisation or capacity.

(ii) How are senior officers and members involved; what mechanisms exist?

E   The Role of `Backbench' Councillors

(i) What are the roles currently played by backbench councils, and how should they be developed? How is the representative role supported?

(ii) How can the representative role of Councillors be enhanced, eg. by giving Councils more to say in decisions affecting their area or by giving groups of Councillors representing a wider area devolved power to take local decisions.

(iii) What is and should be the role of Councillors in scrutinising and evaluating the work of the Council. How should this role be carried out? Where power is delegated to Committees, chairs or officers, should there be watchdog committees or councillors either:

— to scrutinise the propriety of decisions and the value for money achieved by them; or

— to evaluate the quality of service delivery and accessibility of the authorities services from the citizens/consumer point of view; or

— separately, or for other purposes as well.

(iv) Should such a Committee include only elected members; or should there be co-opted members also?

F   Numbers of Councillors

(i) If there was an executive committee would it be necessary to:

(a) Reduce the numbers of Councillors because those excluded from the executive would have less to do? or

(b) Increase the number of councillors to enhance their direct representational role and their role of scrutineers of the executive?

G Payment of Councillors

(i) What problems are their in the present system of payments for Councillors?

(ii) What changes would you like to see:

(a) given the present organisation?

(b) with new forms of organisation?

(iii) Should the Leader of the Council and the Chairman of the Committees receive salaries which reflect their explicit executive roles?

(iv) Should all Councillors receive salaries?

(v) If salaries are ruled out, how could the allowance system be improved to reflect better different levels of responsibility.

(vi) Should Councillors receive allowances for surgeries or local meetings?

(vii) Should there be attendance allowances for informal or party meetings? or for performing single member duties?

H Administrative Support

(i) What present form of administrative support is provided for Councillors. In particular is ward based information provided for Councillors?

(ii) Should all Councillors be provided with increased administrative support, and if so what form of support?

(iii) Should increased administrative support be restricted to:

(a) Leading Councillors where no executive committee exists.

(b) The executive committee.

(c) The executive committee and members of other committees.

(iv) How would this affect the role of councillors and officers?

(v) Is IT support provided? If so, what type? Would better IT provision lesson the need for officer support?

I   Council Manager

(i) What is the Chief Executives role in your authority?

(ii) How does this differ from the Council manager system?

(iii) If there is an executive of elected members should it delegate all management functions to council managers and concentrate only on strategy formulation? How are management functions defined and what about individual cases?

(iv) How long should a council manager be appointed for? The term of one administration?

(v) Should the appointment be a an explicitly political one?

(vi) If the appointment was on 'merit' what safeguards would be required — eg, discipline?

J   The role of minority parties

(i) What effective role would minority's play if the rules of political balance on committees were abandoned and one party committees were allowed to be formed.

(ii) What access do they have now to chief officers? Is there a programme of regular meetings?

(iii) How will access to officers be affected:

(a)   If there is a single party executive group?

(b)   A politically appointed council manager?

(iv) What information should minority parties be denied access to, and in what circumstances?

Annex D

Acknowledgements

D.1 We are grateful to all of the authorities, associations, institutions and individuals who helped us in our work. In particular we are most grateful to the members and officers of the authorities which hosted visits by the task force.

D.2 We would also like to thank the following representatives of INLOGOV for their help:

Professor John Stewart
Professor Kieron Walsh
Steve Leach
Vivien Lowndes
Ken Spencer

D.3 And to thank the councillors who attended the seminar on internal management organised on our behalf by the local authority associations, attended by the then Minister for Local Government, John Redwood. The councillors who attended were:

Association of Metropolitan Authorities

G Bull	Ealing
S Bullock	Lewisham
R Colley	Rochdale
A Colman	Merton
L Duvall	Greenwich
R Farley	Bradford
J Hanham	Kensington and Chelsea
S Keeble	Southwark
G Sutcliffe	Bradford
G Tope	Sutton
R Watson	Sefton

Association of District Councils

H J Brooks	East Cambridgeshire
J Clark	South Somerset
R S Gee	Epsom and Ewell
R Haycraft	South Oxfordshire
S Henig	Lancaster
R Hills	York
E S Jenkins	Bath
M King	Adur
P Soulsby	Leicester
P Starkey	Oxford

Association of County Councils

W Dixon-Smith	Essex
J Ewart	Oxfordshire
J Farrington	Lancashire
J Robertson	Surrey
D Roaf	Oxfordshire
F Whiting	Cornwall

Annex E

Task Force — Visits

The following is a list of the authorities visited by our task force. We are particularly grateful to the members and officers of these authorities for giving us so much of their time, for describing their arrangements so comprehensively, and for answering our questions so openly.

County Councils

Cambridgeshire
Cumbria
Hertfordshire
Lincolnshire
Northumberland

London Boroughs

Croydon
Hammersmith and Fulham
Havering
Islington
Tower Hamlets

Shire Districts

Hertsmere
Lancaster
Middlesbrough
South Somerset
Stroud
The Wrekin

Metropolitan Districts

Kirklees
Leeds

Annex F

Current Framework

F.1   In this Annex we describe the current internal management framework.

Councillors

F.2   The role of the councillor is defined by legislation, in particular by the Local Government Act 1972 and the Local Government and Housing Act 1989. All councillors are elected and take office as representatives of a defined geographical sub-division of the council's jurisdiction. They are all equal, and have the responsibilities of trustees. Certain decisions have to be taken by the council itself — such as approving the budget — but all others may be delegated either to committees or sub committees, or to an officer appointed by the council. Committees with a few statutory exceptions — for example education — can consist only of councillors and must have more than one councillor. Councillors have to be appointed to them in numbers which reflect the relative strengths of their party groups on the council as a whole.

F.3   The role of the committee chair is only legally recognised for procedural purposes and the office of leader is not recognised in statute at all.

Officers

F.4   Officers are employees of, and serve, the whole council. They advise the council and its committees, implement the decisions of the council and may take the decisions which are delegated to them by the council. They cannot sit on decision — making bodies with councillors, and cannot be councillors in their employing council. Most senior officers cannot be councillors anywhere. All officers are legally required to be politically neutral.

The Committee System

F.5   The present committee-based system for discharging council business has evolved over many years and reflects the wide range of functions for which local authorities are responsible. Provisions in the Local Government Act 1972 allow authorities to delegate almost all decisions to a committee, sub-committee or to an officer of the authority. Local authorities in practice operate mainly through a structure of committees and sub-committees which take place on a fixed rota (the committee cycle) culminating in full council meetings every 4-6 weeks. The precise structure varies from one local authority to another but many authorities operate through a number of separate departments which correspond to the committee structure.

The Allowances System

F.6   The remuneration of councillors is based on the principle of voluntary public service, and the purpose of paying allowances to councillors is principally to ensure that:

(1)   they do not suffer financial hardship; and

(2)   a wide range of different types of people are able to stand for membership.

F.7   A new system of allowances was introduced in April 1991. The main aspects of this system are:

— central government limits, by Regulation, the total maximum amount each local authority may spend on councillors allowances, by limiting the amount of allowances it may spend on each councillor. In 1993/94 the following limits were set:

Authority or description of authority	Amount per Councillor £
A county council	3,000
A metropolitan district council	3,000
Each of the following non-metropolitan district councils: Bristol, Cardiff, Derby, Kingston-upon-Hull, Leicester, Luton, Milton Keynes, Northampton, Nottingham, Plymouth, Portsmouth, Southampton, Stockton-on-Tees, Stoke-on-Trent, Swansea, Thamesdown, Warrington, Woodspring	2,115
Any other non-metropolitan district council	1,470
A London borough council	3,000
A joint authority	945
The Council of the Isles of Scilly	1,470

— from the overall amount, calculated by multiplying these sums by the numbers of councillors in each authority, the Secretary of State obliges local authorities to use between 25% and 95% to pay a basic and equal allowance to all councillors and between 5% and 25% on special responsibility allowances for those with special responsibilities — for example the Leader, Deputy Leader, leader of a minority party or chairmen and women of committees;

— the Secretary of State prescribes the maximum amount which may be paid as a special responsibility allowance to a individual councillor: for 1993/94 it was £8,120;

— the Secretary of State specifies which duties a councillor undertakes can qualify for payment of attendance allowances, ruling out payments for constituency meetings, party group meetings and single member duties; and

— within these limits authorities are free to determine the shape of their own scheme of allowances.

Councillors pay income tax on allowance income above the income tax thresholds — except where specific exemptions have been made. Councillors' allowances are taken into account in assessing social security benefits. A councillor loses entitlement to claim unemployment benefit if, after reasonable expenses have been taken into account, he or she receives allowances exceeding £56 per week.

Checks and Balances

F.8 There are a wide range of checks and balances built into the system which are designed to ensure the propriety and accountability of the decision-making process. Similar checks and balances are also in place to ensure the involvement of minority parties and to protect the political neutrality of officers. They are summarised below.

Delegation

F.9 Local authorities have powers to delegate decision-taking. The functions of an authority may be discharged only by a committee, sub-committee or officer of the authority or by the full council. Committees and sub-committees must be politically balanced and there are restrictions on the appointment of co-optees with the voting rights to decision-taking committees.

Access to Information

F.10 Under the provisions of Part VA of the Local Government Act 1972 (inserted by the Local Government Act (Access to Information) Act 1985) councillors have a statutory right of access to all the council papers, with limited exceptions, which may be altered by the Secretary of State, specified in Regulations.

The Audit Commission

F.11 Auditors appointed by the Audit Commission have a responsibility to satisfy themselves of financial propriety on the part of the local authority; and to satisfy themselves that the authority has made appropriate arrangements to secure economy, efficiency and effectiveness in the use of its resources. Auditors also have a role in confirming the legality of actions by local authorities.

The Monitoring Officer

F.12 All Councils must appoint a monitoring officer. The duty of this officer is to report to the full council any cases where he thinks that the council, one of its committees or sub-committees, or one of its officers is about to, or has done something unlawful, improper or which would constitute maladministration.

The Head of the Paid Service

F.13 The Local Government and Housing Act 1989 requires each authority to designate an officer as head of the paid service. The Head of the Paid Service must report as appropriate on the co-ordination of the authority's affairs, levels, grades and organisation of staff, and their appointment and management. The report must go to every member of the authority and be considered by the full authority within three months.

Political Neutrality of Officers

F.14 Following the recommendations of the Widdicombe report, the government extended the restrictions on political activity by local government officers in the Local Government and Housing Act 19889. Employees of a local authority were already disqualified from standing for election in that authority; the 1989 Act extended that disqualification to include employees of another local authority (so-called 'twin-tracking').

The Local Ombudsman

F.15 The local Ombudsman service was established in 1974. It investigates allegations by members of the public that they have suffered injustice as a result of maladministration by a local authority.

The Courts

F.16 Decisions made by local authorities can be challenged in the courts, by judicial review. There are grounds for mounting a challenge, if (*inter alia*) it appears that an authority acted outside its powers or reached a decision that no reasonable authority could have reached.

Inspectorates

F.17 There is a range of inspectorates to ensure that services are delivered legally and efficiently. The distinction can usefully be made between inspection:

(1) to ensure compliance with statutory requirements (enforcement inspectorates); and

(2) to secure, maintain or provide standards of performance (efficiency inspectorate).

The most important areas covered by inspectorates are listed below:-

- ❖ Trading Standards/Consumer Protection
- ❖ Environmental Health
- ❖ Pollution
- ❖ Ancient Monuments and Historic Buildings
- ❖ Planning
- ❖ Building Control
- ❖ Education
- ❖ Police
- ❖ Fire Services
- ❖ Social Work Services

Printed in the United Kingdom for HMSO
Dd296693 9/93 C15 G531 10170